Alison Waines played the cello p[...] making a career change and qualify[...] 1995. Also a qualified teacher, she has designed and presented courses on self-esteem and guided meditation, plus a range of personal development workshops. Her first book, *The Self-Esteem Journal: Using a Journal to Build Self-Esteem*, is also published by Sheldon Press. Alison writes motivational features for a national women's magazine and has made live appearances on television and radio. She lives in Southampton with her husband.

Overcoming Common Problems Series

Selected titles
A full list of titles is available from Sheldon Press,
36 Causton Street, London SW1P 4ST, and on our website at
www.sheldonpress.co.uk

Assertiveness: Step by Step
Dr Windy Dryden and Daniel Constantinou

The Assertiveness Handbook
Mary Hartley

Breaking Free
Carolyn Ainscough and Kay Toon

Calm Down
Paul Hauck

The Candida Diet Book
Karen Brody

Cataract: What You Need to Know
Mark Watts

The Chronic Fatigue Healing Diet
Christine Craggs-Hinton

Cider Vinegar
Margaret Hills

Comfort for Depression
Janet Horwood

Confidence Works
Gladeana McMahon

Coping Successfully with Irritable Bowel
Rosemary Nicol

Coping Successfully with Pain
Neville Shone

Coping Successfully with Panic Attacks
Shirley Trickett

Coping Successfully with Period Problems
Mary-Claire Mason

Coping Successfully with Prostate Cancer
Dr Tom Smith

Coping Successfully with Ulcerative Colitis
Peter Cartwright

Coping Successfully with Your Hiatus Hernia
Dr Tom Smith

Coping with a Stressed Nervous System
Dr Kenneth Hambly and Alice Muir

Coping with Alopecia
Dr Nigel Hunt and Dr Sue McHale

Coping with Anxiety and Depression
Shirley Trickett

Coping with Blushing
Dr Robert Edelmann

Coping with Bowel Cancer
Dr Tom Smith

Coping with Brain Injury
Maggie Rich

Coping with Candida
Shirley Trickett

Coping with Chemotherapy
Dr Terry Priestman

Coping with Childhood Allergies
Jill Eckersley

Coping with Childhood Asthma
Jill Eckersley

Coping with Chronic Fatigue
Trudie Chalder

Coping with Coeliac Disease
Karen Brody

Coping with Cystitis
Caroline Clayton

Coping with Depression and Elation
Patrick McKeon

Coping with Down's Syndrome
Fiona Marshall

Coping with Dyspraxia
Jill Eckersley

Coping with Eczema
Dr Robert Youngson

Coping with Endometriosis
Jo Mears

Coping with Epilepsy
Fiona Marshall and
Dr Pamela Crawford

Coping with Fibroids
Mary-Claire Mason

Coping with Gout
Christine Craggs-Hinton

Coping with Heartburn and Reflux
Dr Tom Smith

Coping with Incontinence
Dr Joan Gomez

Overcoming Common Problems Series

Overcoming Common Problems Series

Living with Crohn's Disease
Dr Joan Gomez

Living with Diabetes
Dr Joan Gomez

Living with Fibromyalgia
Christine Craggs-Hinton

Living with Food Intolerance
Alex Gazzola

Living with Grief
Dr Tony Lake

Living with Heart Disease
Victor Marks, Dr Monica Lewis and
Dr Gerald Lewis

Living with High Blood Pressure
Dr Tom Smith

Living with Hughes Syndrome
Triona Holden

Living with Loss and Grief
Julia Tugendhat

Living with Lupus
Philippa Pigache

Living with Nut Allergies
Karen Evennett

Living with Osteoarthritis
Dr Patricia Gilbert

Living with Osteoporosis
Dr Joan Gomez

Living with Rheumatoid Arthritis
Philippa Pigache

Living with Sjögren's Syndrome
Sue Dyson

Losing a Baby
Sarah Ewing

Losing a Child
Linda Hurcombe

**Make Up or Break Up: Making the Most of
Your Marriage**
Mary Williams

Making Friends with Your Stepchildren
Rosemary Wells

Making Relationships Work
Alison Waines

Overcoming Anger
Dr Windy Dryden

Overcoming Anxiety
Dr Windy Dryden

Overcoming Back Pain
Dr Tom Smith

Overcoming Depression
Dr Windy Dryden and Sarah Opie

Overcoming Impotence
Mary Williams

Overcoming Jealousy
Dr Windy Dryden

**Overcoming Loneliness and Making
Friends**
Márianna Csóti

Overcoming Procrastination
Dr Windy Dryden

Overcoming Shame
Dr Windy Dryden

The PMS Diet Book
Karen Evennett

Rheumatoid Arthritis
Mary-Claire Mason and Dr Elaine Smith

The Self-Esteem Journal
Alison Waines

Shift Your Thinking, Change Your Life
Mo Shapiro

Stress at Work
Mary Hartley

Ten Steps to Positive Living
Dr Windy Dryden

Think Your Way to Happiness
Dr Windy Dryden and Jack Gordon

The Traveller's Good Health Guide
Ted Lankester

**Understanding Obsessions and
Compulsions**
Dr Frank Tallis

When Someone You Love Has Depression
Barbara Baker

Your Man's Health
Fiona Marshall

Overcoming Common Problems

Making Relationships Work
How to Love Others and Yourself

Alison Waines

sheldon PRESS

First published in Great Britain in 2005

Sheldon Press
36 Causton Street
London SW1P 4ST

Copyright © Alison Waines 2005

British Library Cataloguing-in-Publication Data

A catalogue record for this book is available from the British Library

ISBN 0–85969–938–2

1 3 5 7 9 10 8 6 4 2

Typeset by Deltatype Limited, Birkenhead, Merseyside
Printed in Great Britain by
Ashford Colour Press

For Matthew
my amazing husband
who brings me so much enduring happiness
– and for showing me
how brilliantly a relationship
can work.

Thank you to my sister, Ruth,
for forever being my Guardian Angel.

Thank you, too, to all of you who allowed me to walk alongside
you for a while on your troubled journeys – your names and
details have been changed.

Contents

Introduction

About this book

Looking for that elusive 'special' relationship seems to be an ongoing quest for many people today. Have relationships always been so complicated? Throughout history did we endure as much heartache to find the right person, create a relationship that works and make it last a lifetime? Perhaps relationships have always been fraught and complex to some degree, but in current times it seems that relationships are the cause of so much more unhappiness.

As a counsellor, I have worked with many people – male, female, heterosexual, homosexual, bisexual – who tell me they have a history of failed relationships. On the surface these people appear confident and capable and yet they keep getting it 'wrong' when it comes to having a loving, lasting relationship. So is it a matter of 'finding' a great relationship or 'creating' it?

This book is for anyone who wants to find ways to create a successful long-term relationship. It is for anyone who is mystified over why their relationships do not seem to work, or who are wondering if something is wrong with their personality. It is for those who are losing hope that they will ever find someone to share their lives.

If you ask yourself questions like: 'Why do I always choose the wrong type of person?' or 'How come my relationships end so quickly?', then this book will help you find some answers. It is also designed for use by professionals, such as counsellors, who support people struggling through unhappy relationships.

My experience

I believe there are numerous ways we can help ourselves to create better relationships. This view is based on the improvements I have witnessed when working with people through counselling. It is also based on the changes I have been able to make in my own love life. In focusing on relationships and helping people to discover why and how they go wrong, I have discovered many useful principles and I have designed techniques and tools that are included in this book.

1

In my own personal life, I have put these ideas into practice. After a series of relationships that did not work out (and approaching 40), I began to realize that something was wrong. Through developing self-reflection and awareness, I started to understand what was not working and what I needed to do to put things right. You might, like me, have to do some rigorous soul-searching as you work through this book, but if you are serious about improving your love life this can bring enormous rewards.

I got married for the first time in my forties, to someone completely different from most of my previous partners. I had managed to break my cycle of falling (usually) for the wrong kinds of men and to find a relationship where love, affection, honesty, trust, respect, passion, compatibility, warmth, humour and fun are in evidence on a daily basis. For the first time, I can be completely myself in this relationship. This has had a considerable positive effect on my self-esteem and a consequent benefit to the relationship.

Self-esteem

Good self-esteem is essential for healthy relationships. Many of the principles in this book stem from developing and sustaining good self-esteem, as a starting point for reaching out towards others. It works in two ways: first, if you are feeling good about who you are, you are likely to be more attractive to someone who is looking for a healthy relationship. Second, if you prize self-esteem you are more likely to choose someone who values this too and who will help you sustain your self-esteem (and you will move on quickly if they do not).

If you are not able to respect, honour and accept yourself, you will find it difficult to do this with other people. The maxim 'First love yourself before you can love others' is frequently quoted, but in my experience can be confusing. 'How am I to love myself?' I hear people ask, or worse, 'I *don't* love myself, that is why I need someone *else* to love me.' My aim in this book is to show you what 'loving yourself' really means and how, by doing so, you can make your relationships work better. The principles set out in this book not only apply to romantic relationships, but can improve all your relationships, such as with family, friends and colleagues.

Why are relationships so difficult?

In recent years, issues affecting our relationships have changed dramatically. Many factors are present now which never existed before. Women can choose how much time they spend on their careers, and on bringing up a family, so conflicts of roles and responsibilities can cause problems. Feminism seems to have confused both men and women in terms of what is expected of both sexes and what is acceptable behaviour. People are living longer than in the past and can spend 60 years or more with one partner, which can put a strain on a relationship to be continually interesting and absorbing. Modern sexual codes mean that people can choose to have sex without any prospect of a long-term union. So we live in a world with fleeting liaisons born of lust, fantasy and short-term sexual gratification. The outcome is that long-term relationships seem harder to find and more difficult to sustain than ever before.

In romantic relationships too we have a great deal more 'choice' than ever before. It is no longer frowned upon, for example, for people with an extreme age difference to get together, or for couples of the same sex to be partners. In Western cultures, partnerships can now occur across the social spectrum and are not restricted by social class, religion or cultural background. Increased travel and communication mean that we can get to know people from parts of the world that we might never even have heard of in times past. All this choice – and still we are not able to build lasting relationships. If anything, these choices seem to make matters worse for many of us.

You need only take a look at the lonely-hearts sections of magazines to see how many people are looking for a partner these days. Due to the huge demand, wider opportunities have been created to help people find that 'perfect' person. There are agencies for speed-dating, slow-dating, 'no commitment' dating, dinner-dating, lunch-dating, dating based on shared interests, double-dating and extra-marital dating. It seems that even people already in a long-term relationship are looking for a(nother) special person! What are we doing wrong? What are we missing? Are our expectations too high? Instead of finding Mr/Ms Right, should we be settling for Mr/Ms Half-way Decent?

How to use this book

Making Relationships Work is a practical workbook that will take you through a series of steps towards improving your relationships.

INTRODUCTION

To start with you will be investigating what has gone wrong with your liaisons in the past, using a range of reflective pen and paper exercises. You will also be searching for clues as to the hidden influences that shape your choice of partner, your beliefs about what 'love' is, your expectations of a relationship, repeating themes and the ways in which your relationships develop.

This book will show you how to learn from your past and discover recurring and baffling patterns. Exercises will help you to examine the balance of 'power', 'respect' and 'self-esteem' between you and your partner at different stages in your relationship and the impact on each of you when these dynamics shift. You will be shown how to draw up a time-line and cycles of behaviours in your relationships to discover what sabotages them, and you will be offered guidance about breaking these destructive cycles. You will be introduced to principles about the nature of relationships and the part played by self-esteem, together with ideas to build assertiveness. The final section shows you how to become your 'best' self and how to make sure your self-esteem remains high, whether you are in a relationship or not.

Some of the exercises can be completed with a current partner to help you understand each other better; others will be more useful to work through on your own. Along the way, you can read about the insights other people have gained from these exercises and see extracts from their personal journals showing how they struggled to understand themselves and improve their relationships.

If you are reading this book, you may be hoping to resolve some long-standing difficulties. All you need is a simple notebook or private journal to complete the exercises and some time-out for yourself. Hopefully, by the end of the book, you will not only have increased your understanding about yourself and your relationships, but will also have resolved any nagging questions and doubts. Ultimately, my wish is that you can be better prepared to embark on a healthy relationship and can sustain a successful partnership for life with someone special.

1

Why is self-esteem important in relationships?

What is self-esteem?

Self-esteem is a crucial element of all successful relationships and we will return to it at various stages throughout this book. Self-esteem is the way in which we value ourselves and the degree to which we regard ourselves as significant and loveable. Our self-esteem reflects how good we feel about who we are and how we spend our lives. It encompasses our sense of worthiness and our beliefs about our right to participate in all aspects of our existence. Everything we do reflects our levels of self-esteem; our approach to relationships is especially affected and that is why self-esteem is a core theme of this book.

In all areas of our lives, we come across other people and with each one of them we have some kind of 'relationship'. This can range from a casual acquaintance at the bus-stop to an intimate and deep relationship with a partner. There are the on-going relationships we have with our parents, siblings, relatives, children, friends, neighbours and work colleagues. Then the day-to-day encounters we have with a shopkeeper, doctor, postman or strangers we come across in the supermarket. Every time we come into contact with someone our level of self-esteem comes into play.

We do not have an accurate way of measuring self-esteem, but the metaphor of a barometer or thermometer showing a scale from 1 to 10 is a helpful one. Someone with low self-esteem will see themselves as measuring perhaps 2–3 on the self-esteem scale. They are likely to feel inadequate and to act accordingly (for example, by withdrawing from or avoiding other people). For them, a serious commitment to finding ways to build their self-esteem may be the way forward. A person with high self-esteem is likely to score 8–9 on the scale and they might feel more self-assured. Any score somewhere in the middle indicates that our self-esteem could do with a boost.

In relating to others, our inner level of self-esteem is reflected outwardly by our body language, our actions and our means of communication. Take a look at Table 1 which shows some of the identifying features of low and high self-esteem:

Table 1: Features of low and high self-esteem

Low self-esteem	High self-esteem
Little eye contact (feels self-conscious)	Direct eye contact (feels comfortable)
Appears awkward and nervous	Appears secure and relaxed
Hunched shoulders (as though trying to hide)	Shoulders back (happy to be seen)
Anxious fidgeting	Calm and focused
Apologetic about themselves (inadequate)	Celebrating themselves (confident)
Avoids approaching someone they know	Welcomes approaching someone they know

Our outward actions and behaviours usually give away our hidden feelings of self-worth. One useful means of developing self-esteem is through developing assertiveness, because many features are common between high self-esteem and assertiveness. Essentially, assertiveness can help us to develop new behaviours that allow us to feel better about ourselves. Chapter 10 explores assertiveness in greater detail.

Our level of self-esteem is not set in stone at birth. It can and does fluctuate. Outside events and circumstances can affect our self-esteem, such as experiencing loss of self-esteem in response to redundancy. Losing our job in this way can leave us feeling that we have been rejected and that we have nothing to contribute. Conversely, a positive event such as getting married may increase our self-esteem. In this case we feel elated that someone has made a life-long commitment to be our partner. Outside circumstances alone, however, do not determine our self-esteem. Rather, it is our levels of self-esteem that determine the ways we are affected by external events and situations. Someone with low self-esteem who is made redundant, for example, may feel they are not good enough and become disheartened. A person with higher self-esteem may respond differently to the same situation and look more positively at the new opportunities redundancy offers them to develop their skills and find more rewarding work. The same event can therefore produce completely different responses and outcomes according to our levels of self-worth. So why do some people have higher self-esteem than others?

Factors that contribute to self-esteem

One of the strongest influences on our self-esteem is the way others have treated us in the past. For example, a child receiving considerable attention and praise is likely to have higher self-esteem in adulthood than a child who was frequently ignored or criticized.

Furthermore, our levels of self-esteem may vary in different aspects of our lives. Just because we have high self-esteem in one area does not mean we have high self-esteem across the whole spectrum of our lives. For example, June had high self-esteem with regard to her career and work skills, but had low self-esteem when it came to relationships. An extract from June's diary illustrates this:

I was good at school and got top grades. At home the focus was always on how well I had done in exams and essays and everyone thought I was so sure of myself. No one realized that I was very shy and awkward when it came to boys. I didn't feel the least bit confident talking to them. Now I see that my self-esteem was lopsided and it's reflected in how I feel now. Twenty years later, I feel great about myself at work, but my personal life is a mess! (June, maths teacher, 36)

How does self-esteem become established?

During our upbringing, many people have a significant impact on our levels of self-esteem. Parents, teachers, friends, siblings and other family members respond to us in certain ways and each response conveys a message to us about how much they value us. This in turn leads us to draw conclusions about how much we value ourselves. It is as though other people 'teach' us how to regard ourselves. Each time someone responds to us, whether in a positive, neutral or negative way, it is likely to affect our self-esteem. Responses take place through words (and the manner in which the words are spoken), body language (such as a hug, smile, shaking of the head or walking away) or any other kind of response (such as silence). As children, we internalize these responses and subconsciously interpret them to produce beliefs about our own worth.

Tables 2 and 3 give you an idea of how this subconscious interpreting works:

Table 2: The development of low self-esteem

Response of a significant person	Likely belief/impact
Teacher tells you your essay was poor.	'I am not good at what I do.'
Mother ignores you when you want attention.	'I am not worth spending time with.'
Father goes to a football match and leaves you at home.	'I do not deserve to have fun.'
Sister shouts at you.	'I am not loveable.'

Table 3: The development of high self-esteem

Response of a significant person	Likely belief/impact
Teacher tells you your essay was good.	'I am good at what I do.'
Mother reads to you at bedtime.	'I am worth spending time with.'
Father takes you to the fair.	'I deserve to have fun.'
Sister gives you a cuddle.	'I am loveable.'

These tables offer a simplistic view of how this process works, but nevertheless show how the responses of others can start to shape our levels of self-esteem at an early age. What we need to remember is that others' responses are subjective and influenced by many factors. In Table 2, for example, the *real* reason your 'mother ignores you' might be that she is tired or has just had some bad news. Likewise, your 'sister shouts at you' because she is jealous that you were given a better Christmas present. We might interpret these responses to be direct statements about how much we are worth, when in fact they may say more about the other person. Therefore, basing our self-esteem and self-worth on these kinds of responses will always be inaccurate (even though we all do it to some extent) and could lead us to the wrong conclusions about ourselves.

Over time, the beliefs we have interpreted about ourselves start to become part of the internalized 'voice' we all carry around with us and hear over and over in our daily lives. It is the foundation of the self-talk that tells us after a disappointing job interview, for example, that either 'You were useless as usual' (low self-esteem) or 'You did well, you tried your best' (high self-esteem). The more positive our beliefs are about our value, the more likely we are to have high self-esteem. The good news is that if you realize that your self-beliefs have led to low self-esteem, there are steps you can take to address this. In my previous book, *The Self-Esteem Journal: Using a Journal to Build Self-Esteem*, changing your self-talk is discussed in more detail, together with other means of understanding and improving self-esteem. Here, our focus will be on how self-esteem plays a part in affecting relationships.

The impact of low self-esteem on a relationship

Low self-esteem can seriously affect the dynamics in a relationship. The scenarios below give examples of how this can happen:

1 She's too good for me.
Jeff felt inadequate and had low self-esteem. He chose to begin a relationship with Sally. In Jeff's eyes, Sally seemed 'better than' him in every way. Initially he felt he had a great 'catch' in Sally, but very quickly things started to turn sour. Because Jeff saw Sally as better than he was, he inevitably regarded himself as 'less than' her. This left Jeff in a constant state of

insecurity. He asked himself questions like: 'How can I be good enough for Sally?', 'Why did she choose me?', 'What will happen when she finds out what I'm really like?' and 'How long before she meets someone better than me?' All these fears and doubts created an imbalance between them. Sally ended up exerting power over Jeff and then she grew tired of his insecurities. Before long the relationship came to an end.

2 I'm too good for him.

Another person with low self-esteem was Rachel. She, on the other hand, chose to be in a relationship with someone she felt had even less self-esteem than she had. She felt empowered and superior to Gordon and took opportunities to look down on him in order to feel better about herself and try to increase her own low self-esteem. While both partners had low self-esteem, Rachel's desire to gain superiority caused an imbalance between the two of them. Eventually Rachel became bored with Gordon's tendency to be subservient and play the victim, so she ended the relationship.

Perceived 'equality' between partners is a crucial foundation for successful relationships – the sense that you and your partner are equal to each other, and that neither one feels 'less than' or 'better than' the other. Neither Jeff nor Rachel *consciously* chose partners who had a marked difference in self-esteem to their own. Jeff, however, was aware of feeling 'less than' Sally and Rachel was striving to feel 'better than' Gordon. Neither Jeff nor Rachel recognized the inequality they were creating.

This kind of imbalance, where one partner has lower self-esteem than the other, is common and often unrecognized, and it usually has a serious impact on the relationship's success. This is one of the reasons why self-esteem is a significant factor within partnerships. The dynamic of equality will be discussed in further detail in Chapter 6. There will also be an opportunity to explore and measure equality in your own relationships. We will return to the important role played in relationships by self-esteem at further points in this book, but first let us look at some of the ways in which we learn about what love is and how this affects our relationships.

2

What is love?

How we see love

During our childhood, as we are cared for and loved, we build up beliefs about what love is. 'Love' within one family might consist of fights and arguments, so that when a child becomes an adult, he or she may expect conflict or violence to be an integral part of relationships. Love in another family might be based on lots of financial support, but little emotional understanding, so that when a child grows up, he or she finds it hard to be emotionally close, because there is no language or experience for dealing with emotions.

Many of our responses in relationships mirror those from our childhood no matter how removed from family influences we believe or wish we were. Our early experience creates the foundation for subsequent relationships. The ways we see our parents relating to each other and the ways in which they relate to us creates a framework in our minds for what love means to us. Mostly this is a subconscious process, which is one of the reasons why, if we received mixed messages about love when growing up, we can carry on for years experiencing difficulties in relationships that we cannot seem to resolve. It is important to try to bring these subconscious processes to light as far as possible, because without new information to explain our behaviours, it will be very hard to shift problematic patterns.

Ask yourself: What is love? How do you respond? Perhaps you believe that we all mean the same thing when we use the word love in terms of romantic relationships. The statements below show how this is not the case:

Love for me is bound up with 'drama' – my parents had a volatile relationship full of highs and lows. This is how I expect love to be – like being on a roller-coaster ride, and if it isn't full of fights and making-up, then it can't be love. (Jeremy, engineer, 36)

My experience growing up was about looking after myself, because no one seemed to be around much. Dad was on the rigs and Mum sometimes didn't come home until very late, so I learnt that love was about being left to get on with it on your own. (Diane, sports instructor, 24)

My dad died when I was two and my mum poured all her love on to me, as a way of staying close to him, I think. She loved me with a kind of desperation and neediness, so I often felt suffocated. That's how love has always seemed to me. I choose men who are going to need me and depend on me – I can't seem to think of love any other way. (Sherrie, caterer, 29)

Exercise 1: Exploring love in your family

Using a notebook or journal, make some notes as you reflect on the following:

1 Travel back in time and look at the history of 'love' in your family. Think of situations which make you think of love, or how love was shown during your upbringing. Start from as early as you can remember – some family photos might help. Explore the love between your parents and the ways they showed love to you. Think back to weekends and holidays from your childhood, as well as day-to-day scenarios. What were the dynamics in the family that went under the guise of 'love'?

2 Which words do you associate most with the concept of love? Choose from those below, or add your own:

> need, dependency, distance, arguments, fights, violence, making-up, drama, discipline, shouting, anger, physical affection, verbal affection (such as saying 'I love you'), sex, passion, warmth, dominance, interdependence, people-pleasing, obeying, being meek, silences, uncertainty, slammed doors, absence, respect, listening, caring, approval-seeking

3 Think back to when you were about five years old and draw a sketch of your family as though you were taking a snapshot of them on a typical Sunday afternoon (or a time when all the family was present). Use stick-people if that is easier to draw.

4 Take a look at your picture. What associations do you make when you picture your family at home? For example, do you feel a sense of joy and fun or sadness or fear? Is everyone together? Is there harmony? Are people involved with each other or is each person in their own private world? What dynamics are going on that you cannot see, but you know were there? For example, a silent angry atmosphere or having to 'walk on eggshells'.

5 Are there any similarities between the factors you recall about love from your family of origin and your relationships now? Can you name them?

This sort of reflection will help you to see how your unique view of love has been influencing your adult relationships. Self-awareness is the starting point in addressing such issues and is often sufficient in itself to trigger changes.

Developing self-awareness

If you feel that you have a history of relationships that seem to go wrong, time after time, it may be worth investigating this further. Often without realizing, we play out the same patterns of behaviours in our relationships, which lead to the same outcomes. We encounter the same problems over and over again with different partners and nothing seems to get better. We may blame our partners for treating us in unsatisfactory ways, but if we experience a series of relationships where the same kinds of difficulties arise, then the chances are that *we* are doing something that causes or contributes to the problem. By noticing how we behave and respond with our partners, we can discover more about situations we find difficult or which lead to self-sabotaging cycles. Unless we can get clearer about the ways we act and react, we will not be able to make the changes we need for the final result to turn out differently.

In order to get to grips with what goes wrong, we need to develop our self-awareness. This is the mechanism through which we can step back from our habitual behaviours and notice what we do in more detail. Self-awareness is about being conscious of a response or action, when for a long time it may have been subconscious. Self-awareness allows us to shine a torch on our attitudes and ways of being. The simple rule is to notice and not judge – to resist the temptation to put ourselves down or criticize our patterns and habits. Our job is only to observe our behaviours, not condemn them. Most of the time in our lives we are only ever trying to do our best, so we need to develop self-awareness *with kindness* for ourselves, recognizing that we may have been subconsciously maintaining certain behaviours in order to protect or defend ourselves. The new information and understanding we gain through self-awareness, which hitherto has been hidden from us, will offer new perspectives and the scope for change.

A private journal is an excellent way to record your self-awareness and the new insights you discover. You might want to focus first, for example, on the 'problem areas' in your relationships and note down which common themes emerge. Try to stand back and observe what happens in situations that repeatedly cause you suffering in your relationships.

Lisa explains her first attempts at exploring her behaviour using self-awareness:

I used my journal to record what I noticed about myself with Jon. I began to see that I often said what I thought he wanted to hear, rather than what I really felt. I knew, for example, when he told me he was going away for the week with his friends, that I felt hurt and yet I heard myself saying 'yes, no problem' without hesitation! I started to see how I trapped myself into patterns of approval-seeking, instead of stating what I really wanted. (Lisa, choreographer, 24)

At first, you will probably start to notice behaviours only *after* the event has occurred. Ultimately, however, once you realize that a habitual behaviour is causing you long-term problems, your awareness of it *at the time of doing it* will enable you to stop, take a breath and give you a moment to reconsider your response. This kind of awareness during the actual moment itself may take some practice, but if mastered it can be helpful in breaking certain patterns.

Lisa went on to describe how she used her self-awareness to help her:

When I realized that it was me who was causing my own problems with Jon, I decided to do something about it. By practising being more aware and anticipating difficult situations,

14

I was able to react differently. When Jon told me he was going to a friend's wedding on his own, I didn't say 'OK' straight away. I was aware of how easy it would have been to bite my tongue and pretend to be fine about it, but my awareness sent a little alarm bell ringing in my head. Instead, I said that I felt hurt that he hadn't thought of asking me to go with him to the wedding. There was a long silence and I felt scared, but in the end we had a long talk about commitment and it has helped get things clearer for both of us. I felt very proud of myself for breaking a pattern.

In the above extract Lisa was able, through self-awareness, to challenge and change some of her habitual behaviours. By having a clearer picture of the kind of destructive patterns you seem to 'drift' into, you can focus on the areas that need addressing.

Exercise 2: Developing self-awareness

1 Start by making a list of the areas in your relationships that typically lead to arguments or never seem to get resolved. They may involve situations around sex, being with other people, jealousy, possessiveness, commitment, the influence of parents, money, starting a family and so on.

2 Then, over the coming days or weeks, use your self-awareness to notice when these situations arise again and what happens. Notice how a problem begins, who says or does what, and how the scenario unfolds.

3 Record what happens in detail as though you were an objective observer.

4 Keep hold of your notes, as they will be useful for Exercise 4 in Chapter 3.

Hidden influences

The self-awareness required to identify recurring problems will help you to see other aspects of your relationships, which may have been hidden from you up to this point. When you take an overview of this and previous relationships do you see any broader patterns that repeat? Do you find yourself attracted to the same kinds of people, who ultimately let you down or damage your self-esteem? Do you find yourself ending a relationship out of some overwhelming panic you do not understand, or do you watch yourself playing out all kinds of strange 'games' with your partner?

If these kinds of dynamics are happening to you, it may be that there are some hidden influences from your past affecting your judgement or playing a part in your behaviour. The exercise below may help you to go beneath the surface to access some of these subconscious processes.

Exercise 3: Tracing the influences

1 Write down the names of all the key people with whom you have had romantic relationships on separate lines along the edge of a page. Leave a few lines underneath each name. Along the top of the page write five column headings: Start, Middle, End, Overview and Age.

2 Taking each relationship in turn, reflect on how each one began and make a brief note under 'Start'. This might include the circumstances in which you met, or the way in which you got together, such as: 'Met at a bar – had too much to drink' or 'She showed interest in me so I tagged along'.

3 Then remember a time during the course of the relationship once things were a little more established. Write down a few notes here under 'Middle'. This might look something like: 'Started to feel insecure' or 'Lots of fun – but it didn't go much deeper than that'.

4 Under 'End' write down the way in which the relationship ended. Did you or your partner end it? Did it drag on long after the flame had burned out? Was it an amicable and mutual decision? Did it end several times and start up again? Did it end because of someone else or other circumstances?

5 Look back to the time spent with that person and write down a few words which sum up that relationship under 'Overview', such as: 'Went on too long', 'Should have stayed friends', 'I always felt second-rate', 'She was too interested in her career', 'He was preoccupied with having children' and so on.

6 In the last column, consider the mental and emotional 'age' you felt most often during this relationship. Even though you would have actually been a teenager or an adult, you may have responded in child-like ways in the relationship, representing earlier experiences. For example: 'I felt about six years old – I was always trying to please and be a good girl' or 'I felt about 14 years old – trying to be offhand and independent'.

7 Once you have filled in the details for each partner, see which themes emerge. Are there any aspects of the relationships that repeat? Do any factors seem unhealthy now that you reflect on them? Did you feel pulled into scenarios which you knew were destructive? If you answered yes to these questions, you are likely to be responding to influences from your past.

Finding themes in relationships

Our relationship with our parents (or prime carers) is our first taste of being 'in a relationship' and this invariably plays a part in our later relationships, when we are older. Being with our parents as a child is our first experience of 'love' and without realizing we often aim to repeat the flavour of this experience, because there is something familiar about it. Sometimes the experiences were not healthy for us, but we may still try to replicate them in our adult encounters (albeit subconsciously), because they feel like known and safe ground.

Phil discovered this when he explored the themes in his relationships. This is an extract from his journal:

When I had written down the details of all my relationships, I could see that there were themes that were repeating time after time. I always got to the stage with girlfriends where I would do anything to stay in the relationship, even when the evidence was mounting up that it wasn't really working any more. I had this real dread of it finishing and a bigger dread of ending up alone. When I reflected on this, I remembered when I was three that my mother had a prolonged period in hospital during the birth of my brother. I remember feeling completely lost and abandoned when

17

she disappeared suddenly. When she came back, my baby brother was taking up all her attention. I felt left out. I used to hold on to her apron whenever she looked like she was going to leave the house and I feel agitated even now as I recall this. (Phil, publisher, 35)

Phil came across these memories because he realized that when he thought about how old he felt during most of his relationships, he kept coming back to an age of about three. His fears of being left alone, which originated during that childhood incident, were still being played out during his adult relationships. He could now understand why he found it so hard to end a relationship and why feelings of panic arose at the thought of being on his own.

Phil was able to do more exploration and to move on from this dynamic. As well as understanding more about what he felt, he was able to visualize the little boy of three and imagine being a loving parent to himself at that age when feelings of fear arose. He found he could relate with empathy to the child part of himself and also to the adult part struggling to come to terms with the dread of abandonment. This helped him to acknowledge those feelings more openly, rather than feel confused and pathetic. He started to realize that he had resources and strengths as an adult, which he did not have as a child. Once he could separate the impact of the past from his current life, he could see that being alone, in reality, was not the terrifying experience he feared. As a result, Phil was able to take more control of the outcome of his relationships and no longer felt pulled into the same repeating patterns.

If you feel that you regress to a younger age in relationships, you may find it useful to look for clues in your memories associated with that age. In doing so you will be finding out if earlier events are playing a hidden part in your adult interactions. It may help to find photographs of yourself and your family at the age you feel yourself slipping back to. Any strong associated feelings could be affecting your relationships in the present. As Phil did, you may find it helpful to separate those feelings, belonging to the child part of you, from those which feel like genuine adult responses. Child-like responses are often characterized by over-reactions; extremes or fear, hurt or anger, even tantrums. By acknowledging and taking care of these feelings you will be starting to move on.

3

Where do your relationships go wrong?

In this chapter we will be taking self-awareness (as explained in Chapter 2) one step further. We will be identifying the self-sabotaging patterns that we tend to repeat in relationships and will be putting them down on paper. Sometimes it is hard for us to separate our part in a situation from the reactions of other people, and in a difficult situation (like an argument) it is not easy to remember what happened as emotions are running high.

Cycles of behaviours

The exercise below will help you to plot the sequence of events as they occur in any awkward or problematic situation. It will help you to notice how you tend to react to your partner and what they then do or say in return. By drawing a diagram to show the sequence of responses between you, you should gain more clarity. In doing so, you will be able to distinguish the different stages of your interactions, see how you keep falling into the same behaviours and then do something about changing them. You can draw up a cycle for any kind of relationship, such as with a parent or child, as well as with a romantic partner.

Exercise 4: Drawing the cycle

1 In this exercise, try to separate the sequence of events you experience into single steps. Within the relationship you wish to explore, first of all try to define the starting point of an awkward scenario. Using your notes from the self-awareness exercise in the last chapter (Exercise 2), look for the point that signals the beginning of a familiar cycle. Call this starting point 'A'. Your starting point could be anything that sets off the awkward scenario. It could be something your partner says, or does (or does *not* do), or the manner in which they say or do something that is the trigger.

2 Draw a circle similar to the one in Figure 1, and write down what happens at your starting point A, together with a brief description of

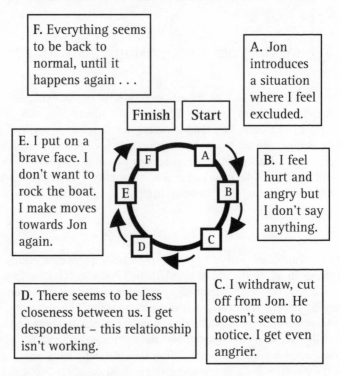

Figure 1: Lisa's cycle of behaviour

how you feel and how you react at this point. (The example shown in Figure 1 builds on Lisa's first experiences of self-awareness in her relationship with Jon – see her journal extract in the previous chapter.)

3 Starting at A, what happens next? What does this first step usually lead to? Label this 'B' and again add what happens and how you feel and react.

4 Keep asking 'What happens next?' until you have completed every stage of your cycle (you may have more or fewer steps in your cycle than Lisa). What is the end result? The final result will often leave you in a position for the cycle to start all over again at another time. This is the tiresome 'back to square one' feeling that leaves you realizing that nothing has changed.

Once you have drawn up your cycle, notice the next time this cycle

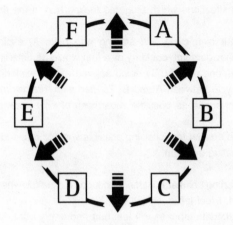

Figure 2: Points where the cycle can be broken

repeats. When it does, you can check if all the steps take place in the same order as your diagram. Did you miss out any steps? Do you need to modify your cycle to include more detail?

Breaking the cycle

The next stage is to consider ways of breaking this cycle. Often the cycles are destructive to our self-esteem. They cause us to feel unhappy and to doubt ourselves and the relationship. They keep repeating because we do nothing different to change the cycle of events and responses. Breaking the cycle means reacting in a new way, a way that avoids the discomfort or pain of our habitual reactions. Breaking the cycle can take place between any of the points on the circle. For example, after event A has taken place, you can do something different so that B does not take place. If B takes place, you can do something different to prevent C from taking place and so on. In Lisa's cycle there are six opportunities to break the cycle reflecting the spaces between the six activating events, A–F. In Figure 2 the arrows show all the points where new responses or behaviours could break the cycle to give rise to a more satisfactory conclusion.

1 Consider first what it is you want to avoid or achieve by doing something different. Lisa wanted to avoid her feelings of hurt escalating into anger and then avoid the pretence that everything was fine in the relationship. She wanted her hurt to be acknowledged, and ideally prevent the situations which triggered feeling hurt in the first place.

2 Using your own cycle and starting with point A, explore all the possible behaviours you could try at A that would be different from the way you respond usually. By doing so, you will be exploring ways to break the cycle between A and B. To start with, brainstorm as many different responses as possible regardless of how appropriate they seem.

Lisa came up with the following possible ways to respond differently to her activating event at A.

Lisa's starting point at A = 'Jon introduces a situation where I feel excluded. I feel left out.'
Lisa's habitual response = 'I feel hurt and angry but I don't say anything.'

Possible new responses:
(a) Get angry with Jon and tell him his behaviour of excluding me is unacceptable.
(b) Get a friend to tell him it is not acceptable.
(c) Exclude Jon – go out with my own friends to get even.
(d) Get involved with someone else – and then end the relationship with Jon.
(e) End the relationship with Jon if he excludes me again.
(f) Do something to make Jon jealous.
(g) Tell Jon how I feel – that I feel hurt when he excludes me (the one Lisa ultimately chooses).

3 Use this same technique to explore new ways of reacting for each point on your cycle, between B and C, C and D and so on. You will then have a multitude of possible strategies for preventing this cycle from recurring and you can then choose the ones that feel most suitable.

4 Before Lisa chose to try a new response, she imagined the consequences of each one and how effective it might be. She did not want to create another cycle worse than the original one! This will be important for you to do too, so that you take full responsibility for the new behaviour you choose and also have an idea of the outcome you expect or hope for. Take each new possible reaction and, in your mind, imagine where it might lead and how the other person might respond.

Do not forget that you cannot change another person's behaviour, but you can let them know the effect it has on you and ask for what you need.

5 Reflect on self-esteem, equality, respect and honesty with regard to each of your possible choices. If you choose a particular response will it be done with integrity? Will it damage your self-esteem? Will you feel a worthy person for doing it?

Lisa evaluated her responses and chose the final one ((g) above), because although it was a risk to reveal her true feelings, this response was honest and ultimately she wanted a relationship where honesty played a major part. In this way it best met the end she was trying to achieve.

6 Once you have selected a response, make a note to yourself. Next time the cycle reappears, see if you can put the new behaviour into practice.

7 You may find that your diagram has links with similar cycles in this or other relationships. This means that you can use ideas from your work on this cycle to help resolve a range of related difficulties, either with your partner or with other people.

Changing habitual responses in order to break a destructive cycle is not always easy. It may take a lot of practice and courage to try something new. You may not be ready to do anything different straight away or you may be prevented from acting differently out of fear of losing the relationship. There will come a point, however, when the pain of revisiting the same old distressing scenario is likely to outweigh the fear of putting the relationship at risk. You may find you get to the stage where you cannot bear to go through the same destructive cycle any more and that will be the time to put these ideas into practice.

The stages of love

Love goes through several stages in the development of a relationship and knowing these stages can shed some light on how we are feeling and the direction we are going in.

The 'in-love' phase is usually the first phase. This is where we first feel sexual attraction and a desire for physical closeness with our partner. To be in love usually means feeling intense overwhelming feelings of romantic desire for someone. We may want to be holding hands, gazing into each other's eyes and sharing long telephone conversations. In purely biological terms, this is the stage intended for human beings to procreate and it often lasts up to 18 months. For our ancestors, this was sufficient time for a man and woman to meet, be attracted, have sexual intercourse, sustain a nine-month pregnancy and provide for the early months of the baby's life. After this time, in evolutionary terms there is no further necessity for the 'in-love' phase within that partnership. Nature has done its job and the population has been increased!

For us today, this 'in-love' phase often influences the length of a romantic relationship. Many relationships falter around the 18-month mark and come to an end. This is the point at which our potent feelings of passion may fade and we might be starting to see our partner for the first time without rose-tinted glasses. Our lover's quirky habits, the ones we delighted in at the start, can now become irritations! This is the 'in-love' phase drawing to a close. If the relationship is to succeed beyond this point, the 'in-love' feelings will need to be enhanced by a deeper love, which reflects a longer-term bond of intimacy and caring for each other.

As a rough guide, several of the factors associated with the 'in-love' and 'deeper love' stages are outlined below. This may help you to judge the stage you are at in your own relationship, or the stages you have reached in previous ones:

The in-love experience:
Sexual attraction, passion, desire, excitement, longing, affection, physical contact, fantasy, being spell-bound and preoccupied, nervousness, trying to make a good impression, being on one's best behaviour, attention to appearance and hygiene, exploring each other emotionally, mentally and physically . . .

The deeper-love experience:
All of the above (often to a lesser extent) plus: caring, empathy, respect, honesty, emotional intimacy, sharing experiences, psychological support, negotiating, arguing, compromising, companionship, friendship, being oneself more (less attempt at trying to impress), acceptance of the other person's shortcomings . . .

In the next chapter we will be investigating your past and current relationships in more detail to assess how well they have been working.

4

Assessing your relationships

By now you are likely to be gaining some important insights into the patterns in your relationships, as you reflect on and begin to collect crucial information about the history of your past liaisons. In this chapter we will be assessing how well your relationships work and how your self-esteem is, or has been, affected.

Rating your self-esteem in relationships

We start by rating your self-esteem in your current or previous partnerships. Measuring self-esteem is a useful tool in determining how well a relationship works. If being in a relationship causes your self-esteem to diminish, then it is not healthy for you. Conversely, if being with someone helps your self-esteem to flourish, then the relationship is working well. Good relationships will normally foster high self-esteem in both parties, because the dynamics are such that each person feels confident about being who they really are. The relationship allows each person to feel valued and appreciated, and have the sense that they are genuinely contributing something positive to the other person.

Outside circumstances, as well as changes within the dynamics of the relationship, can affect our self-esteem and sense of power and control. The impact of 'life-events' (such as redundancy, bereavement and infertility) on the power dynamic between partners is explored later in Chapter 6. In this chapter we will isolate changes *within* the relationship (rather than external events) that may affect self-esteem. The following exercise will help you to assess the ways in which self-esteem has fluctuated during the history of your relationships.

Exercise 5: The self-esteem time-line

1 Refer to Figure 3. Taking a sheet of paper, draw a dot at the top left-hand corner and label this 'Start'. This represents the beginning of the relationship you wish to explore. Recall how you felt *just before* you began this relationship and rate your self-esteem at that time. Use the

26

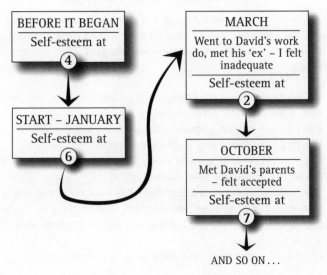

Figure 3: The self-esteem time-line

scale of 1 to 10, where 1 = your self-esteem was poor and 10 = your self-esteem was excellent. Just before your starting point, write the words 'before it began' and note down your self-esteem rating at that time.

2 Now using the same scale of 1 to 10, at 'Start' note down the level of your self-esteem at the beginning of the relationship. This would be during the early days when you were starting to get to know each other.

3 Then consider how your self-esteem fluctuated from then on during the course of the entire relationship. Weave your way down the page, drawing your time-line. Note down any significant dates, milestones and turning points that occurred between you that had an impact on your self-esteem, together with the rating you would give yourself at that time.

4 Continue to write down noteworthy dates on your time-line, together with your self-esteem rating at each point until you reach either the end of the relationship or the present time.

27

5 You should now have a map of the changes in your self-esteem during the entire relationship. Look for patterns and clues to help you see where and why your self-esteem has changed. Then answer the following:

- Did your self-esteem start high and gradually get lower and lower due to the dynamics between you?
- Did your self-esteem gradually improve during the relationship?
- Did your self-esteem stay relatively the same?
- Did your self-esteem fluctuate widely in extremes between high to low or vice versa (the 'roller-coaster' effect)?
- Was there anything in particular about this relationship that had an adverse effect on your self-esteem (such as not being able to trust your partner, lack of respect between you, possessiveness, jealousy and so on)?
- Overall, was this relationship good for your self-esteem?

Generally, if a relationship is healthy for you and going to help you develop, you need to feel that your self-esteem blossoms with the other person more often than it declines. If, by being in a certain relationship, you feel that you are always struggling to maintain your self-esteem, then there is either a power dynamic between you that needs adjusting (see Chapter 6), or you need to find another relationship where your self-esteem does not suffer.

Tracking the history of self-esteem in a relationship is just one way of checking how well it works for you. In the next section, we look further at the dynamics between partners.

Four types of dependency

In relationships we often find ourselves playing out an unconscious dynamic concerning levels of dependency. When we are growing up, love is bound up with dependency and we go through several stages before adulthood (the 'terrible twos' and adolescence being the major ones) which help us to explore the balance between dependence and independence.

The 'terrible twos' describes a period when a child has gained a great deal of independence since birth. A newborn baby is wholly reliant on a parent for food, care and entertainment, whereas toddlers can now walk by themselves, feed themselves, communicate in more detail and be understood. They can ask for things, say 'no' and wander off to play on their own. Children of this age are learning what it is like to do things for themselves. They want to test their boundaries and often rebel against support and help from a parent. This testing out of independence and will-power is a necessary stage in growing up.

In a similar way, adolescence embodies another period of exploring independence. Teenagers are learning to make their own decisions, to break away from the traditions of the family, and they often react against the values of their parents. In evolutionary terms this is an essential step – a way of preparing to separate from parents in order to embark on adulthood.

Having reached adulthood, there are situations and dynamics that can affect the balance of dependence and independence in relationships. When the level of dependence is out of balance it can cause difficulties, such as when one partner becomes too dependent on another, or when a partner is unable to 'commit'. Take a look at Figure 4, which shows four major types of dependency that occur.

1 Dependence

Complete dependence in a relationship is typified by the relationship between mother and baby. Babies depend on their mother (or carer) for all their needs to be met and would not survive if left on their own. In an adult relationship this level of dependence is not normally healthy, unless it is due to the ill-health, old age or disability of a partner. In such circumstances there may be a conscious agreement that one person will need to lean heavily on the other on a short- or long-term basis, in order to survive.

There will always be times in a relationship when the dependency of one person might increase temporarily, caused by circumstances such as a broken limb, temporary ill-health, redundancy, pregnancy, bereavement and so on. The balance can then be adjusted once the crisis is over. If this can work equally well for both partners in the relationship, it creates a secure foundation for mutual support. In the long term, however, where both people are fit and healthy, over-dependency of one partner on the other can be problematic. Some people, for example, deliberately choose 'needy' partners to ensure this person will rely on them, be indebted to them and never leave. This sets up a 'parent/child' type of relationship, where the needy person becomes a 'child who never grows up' and who feels incapable without the other person. Where such inequality is

1. Dependent	2. Co-dependent

Basic message is:	'I need you'. 'I might not survive, without you'.	'I need you to complete me'. 'I can't live without you'. 'You must be there for me'. 'We are one and the same'.
Healthy in:	Parent and child carer with a sick or disabled person.	Never healthy (claustrophobic, trapping, but makes you feel needed).

3. Independent	4. Interdependent

Basic message is:	'We are separate'. 'We grow as individuals'.	'We are individuals, but share much of our lives'. 'We enjoy doing things together and we also have our own interests and identities'. 'I would be shocked and upset, but I will survive without you'.
Healthy in:	Friends, parent with an adolescent son or daughter, colleagues at work.	Loving relationships.

Figure 4: Four types of dependency

established between partners, it is unlikely that a sustainable relationship will survive in the long term.

2 Co-dependence

Co-dependence is never healthy and, like dependency, is based on the need to be needed, although often in a more subtle or subconscious form. Co-dependence is usually established when someone is drawn to a partner they think they can 'help' or 'change' (such as with an alcohol-dependent person or drug-user). Because this is usually unacknowledged it is never addressed. An example of this type of scenario is the relationship between Barry and Sam.

Barry is on the look-out (perhaps subconsciously) for a relationship that he can turn into a mission to 'cure' the other person. Instead of equality (with the inevitable shifts in needs between partners), Barry takes on the role of 'martyr' and tries to heal Sam (a drug-user), who slips into a 'victim' role. Barry seems to be waiting for Sam's problems to improve, but because Sam has someone to love him and accept him as he is, he always gives up on his treatment programme. Barry may not realize that he is enabling Sam to continue to be an addict. Neither can imagine a relationship without this dynamic. Barry needs to be needed and if Sam had a full recovery, Barry's role would have to change. He does not know any other way to be in a relationship. Sam wants a relationship that enables his drug habit to continue and as long as Barry is always there for him no matter what, he feels safe enough to carry on without changing anything. The relationship therefore becomes stuck and never moves beyond co-dependency.

3 Independence

Independence encompasses self-sufficiency, self-reliance, autonomy and freedom, and is appropriate in many adult relationships, such as between friends, siblings and colleagues. It can cause problems in close relationships when a partner cannot be anything other than independent and feels unable to trust or commit. In this way, independence can block intimacy and stop a relationship from deepening. For example, Kay found that her fear of being hurt was so great that she maintained an independent stance in all her relationships. Her latest partner, Chris, was starting to lose interest because Kay would not consider moving in with him, often 'forgot' to answer his calls, and was leading Chris to believe that he was not important to her.

31

A certain level of independence is important in healthy relationships (see Interdependence, below), but not when independence is the *only* way of being.

4 Interdependence

Interdependence is regarded as the most healthy approach in close relationships. It allows both parties to have a level of independence *and* dependence. Each partner has parts of their lives they share together and parts that they pursue on their own.

For Teddy and Les, this means that they share some mutual friends, but they each have other friends who do not know them as a couple. Teddy loves golf and Les loves tennis, so they enjoy these activities separately. French cinema is a love they share, so they see films together. The interdependent dynamic allows each of them to grow as individuals and fulfil their own dreams and potential, while also sharing a great deal of intimacy. Each brings interest into the relationship from the encounters and experiences they have as individuals.

Try the following exercise:

Exercise 6: Four types of dependence

1 Which style of dependence do you recognize from your current or most recent relationship?

2 Have most of your relationships been built on the same dynamic?

3 Where in your life do you see a role-model for this type of dependence? Think about your parents' relationship, or other relationships that might have influenced you.

4 Are you happy with the kind of dependence you experience in your relationships? Is it destructive in any way? Could it lead to resentment? Are you putting your own life on hold for someone else? Do your relationships only ever go so far? Do you avoid intimacy?

5 Would you like to change anything, or ask for some changes from your partner? If so, you may need to raise this issue with your partner and discuss any changes you would like to make between you.

If you feel that you are entrenched in behaving in an inappropriate dependent, co-dependent or independent way, and cannot foresee being able to address this on your own, you may need more long-term help and support than this book can offer. See Suggested Reading or find a counsellor you can work with on this issue (details are given at the end of this book). For most of us, however, recognizing and understanding the reality of the situation can open our eyes and lead us to make the changes we wish for.

Core beliefs about relationships

The kinds of relationships we choose are in line with our beliefs about ourselves and our self-esteem. These beliefs create our subconscious 'map' and we usually choose scenarios that fit this internal map. The first step in changing the kinds of relationships we have is to examine our 'core beliefs' about relationships – the ones that form the foundation of our internal map. We need to know what our beliefs are to see whether they are getting in the way of creating successful relationships. If we can change the map, we can change the experiences we have.

Hidden beliefs about who we are and what we deserve can lead us to choose partners who are harmful or unsuitable for us, and we may repeat this time after time. If so, these beliefs need to be changed. For example, someone who believes 'I am not worthy of love' will create relationships where love does not come easily, and where forms of abuse might become acceptable. Someone afraid of being hurt may subconsciously sabotage the relationship, to end it before their partner does. In contrast, someone who believes 'I am a worthy and loving person' will create relationships that fit this belief. They will choose partners who treat them with respect and love (and if not, will end the relationship).

Exercise 7: Your core beliefs about relationships

Using your journal, complete the following in as many words as you need:

1 I tend to expect relationships to be . . .
2 All my relationships are . . .
3 In relationships I always feel I need to . . .

4 In relationships I believe these things about myself . . .
5 In relationships I must never . . .
6 I usually choose partners who are . . .
7 In relationships I tend to behave/become . . .
8 In relationships I feel safe when . . .
9 I feel unsafe when . . .
10 I cannot imagine a relationship where . . .
11 I would love to have a relationship where . . .
12 I think relationships should be about . . .

Below is a list of 'healthy' responses to these questions, outlining core beliefs that are likely (as long as the other person also has healthy core beliefs) to result in good relationships. These are not definitive responses and many others will be equally healthy, but it may be useful as a guide to see how your own statements compare:

1 I tend to expect relationships to be based on equality and a deep caring and affection for each other.
2 All my relationships are based on respect, interdependence, sharing and love.
3 In relationships I always feel I need to be completely myself.
4 In relationships I believe these things about myself: that I am worthy of being loved and that my love is worth having.
5 In relationships I must never keep quiet when things are bothering me, or pretend everything is OK when it is not.
6 I usually choose partners who are emotionally stable, warm, who have time for me and are able to commit.
7 In relationships I tend to behave with more confidence to develop my individual strengths and interests, because I have the stable foundation of the relationship.
8 In relationships I feel safe when we talk a lot about important issues between us.
9 I feel unsafe when things are not being said.
10 I cannot imagine a relationship where there is abuse or intentional hurt, or where important issues are never addressed.
11 I would love to have a relationship where I can express all that I am and encourage my partner to do the same.
12 I think relationships should be about feeling secure, loved and prized and offering these qualities to the other person, so that we can both grow and blossom in our unique ways.

You will notice that the significant themes of healthy core beliefs are self-esteem, honesty, respect, equality, interdependence and being able to be oneself. These themes are central to this book and each one is explored at various points throughout the text, so that you can understand their importance and develop them for yourself.

Denise made the following discoveries when she addressed her core beliefs:

> *When I completed the questionnaire I realized how much I was hiding my real self in my relationships. I always expected relationships to be 'difficult' and I felt I had to be capable and never complain. I needed constant reassurances, but no matter how many times I heard 'I love you' it wasn't enough. I felt insecure and was always expecting it to go wrong. (Denise, resources manager, 25)*

After more reflection on the core beliefs she wanted to have, Denise stated the following:

> *I knew I had to modify my beliefs if I was ever going to have a relationship that worked! One of the areas I tried to tackle first was honesty. I decided to risk being myself more and I actually allowed my current boyfriend to see me cry. I thought he'd go right off me, but he was great. It has helped him to own up to some of his problems too. We talk more now. It has given me confidence to see that he still likes me, warts and all.*

Exercise 8: Reflecting on your core beliefs

1 How many of your responses in Exercise 7 were 'healthy' ones?

2 Which of your responses seemed the least 'healthy'?

3 In which area of your relationships would you like to change your attitudes?

4 What would you *like* your answers to the questions in Exercise 7 to have been? (Answer them all again if you wish, from this perspective.)

5 What would you have to do, think or believe differently to have more 'healthy' core beliefs?

6 What small thing could you start to change about your beliefs *right now*?

In the next chapter we will be exploring how your subconscious is programming the kinds of partners you choose.

5

Revealing your patterns

The partners you choose

As we have seen, our choice of partners is influenced by our core beliefs and also by our upbringing. This chapter will give you some ideas about reviewing what you look for in someone and the kinds of places you expect to find potential partners, as well as offering some pointers towards developing better relationships.

Subconscious forces, such as our core beliefs, may lead us to search for certain kinds of people or to maintain patterns that steer us towards the same conclusions. There are other subconscious forces, however, that can cause us to create a particular dynamic. We may be completely unaware, for example, that in our current relationships we are recreating feelings and atmospheres that were present in our family when we were children. We will explore three of these hidden forces here: the drive to 'mirror', the drive to 'avoid' and the drive to 'replicate'. We will also look at a subconscious force particularly associated with low self-esteem, the drive to 'complete'.

The drive to mirror

The most commonly reported force influencing our choice of partner is that of finding ourselves attracted to someone who reminds us of our same-sex or opposite-sex parent. This is the drive to mirror what we have already experienced in the past. If a parent was shy, distant and unavailable, for example, a son or daughter may look for this in a partner. Likewise if a parent was doting, a son or daughter might seek a partner who will spoil them and make them feel special. A child from a family with an alcoholic parent may find a partner in later life who is substance-dependent. Familiarity is the feature of the drive to mirror – people seek to copy an early 'love' experience that they already know, even when it may not be the most healthy experience for them.

The drive to avoid

Another subconscious drive in finding a partner involves *avoiding* characteristics of a parent. For example, Annie and Paul are brother and sister. Their mother was smothering and invasive, and neither can bear it when potential partners are overbearing with them. They are attracted to the opposite: men and women who are self-contained and independent.

The drive to replicate

'Replicators' tend not to look for a dominant parental quality in a partner, but *take on* this quality themselves. Nick, for example, had a mother who took on the role of martyr in the family, being there for others and neglecting herself. In his relationships, Nick found himself replicating this approach, choosing partners who were in need of special care, such as recovering addicts.

The drive to complete

If we have low self-esteem and feel that we are not 'good enough' or complete in ourselves, we may look for another person to 'complete' us – a person who possesses those qualities we admire or aspire to. Instead of working on developing those qualities in ourselves, we try to find them in someone else, often putting them on a pedestal.

The problem with 'pedestal relationships' is that there will never be equality between partners – one of the key factors that helps a relationship work. As we saw at the end of Chapter 1, with this kind of inequality one person will always be in awe of, or feel 'less than', the other. In healthy relationships, the balance of need and power will tend to swing, so that at any point either partner can expect or provide extra support (such as following a period of depression or illness). With pedestal relationships, because the one on the pedestal has been given more permanent power, this natural swing gets blocked. The likely scenario is that the person with low self-esteem constantly lives in fear of losing the person they have put on the pedestal, so they do everything they can to keep that person happy and interested. By seeking to please in this way, they are likely to lose their sense of self and become more and more dependent on their partner, their self-esteem ebbing away all the time.

Usually the most successful relationships are those where each person has a strong sense of self and does not need the other person to 'complete' them. Each one knows they can survive and be whole in the world without the other person; their partner is not a prop holding them up or defining who they are.

The next exercise helps you to review your upbringing and discover which dominant drive may play a part in your choice of partners.

Exercise 9: What is driving your choice of partners?

Use your journal to explore these questions:

1 Using a large sheet of paper, write 'Mother' and 'Father' (or the names of the people who were your main carers) at the top of two separate columns. Reflect on the dominant characteristics of each of your parents and their roles within the family. What is the first thing you think about when you bring each parent to mind? Write down some key words to describe the most common behaviour of each parent – the following list may help:

> lack of concern for you, over-concern, criticism, kindness, not being available for you, being emotionally aloof, generous, giving too much advice (controlling), overbearing, over-praising, being needy or dependent on you, being jealous, doting, neglectful

2 Now examine both columns. Do you look for any of these qualities in a partner (mirror)? Or do you steer clear of them altogether (avoid)? Do you take on any of these qualities yourself (replicate)? Consider these questions with regard to each parent.

3 When you look for a partner, are you drawn to qualities you admire and would dearly love to have as part of your own personality (the drive to complete)?

4 Are you influenced in your relationships by any significant incidents in your family during your upbringing? For example, do you find it hard to trust that people will not leave you because a parent died? Do you test partners to see if they love you enough, because a parent abandoned the family?

5 Consider how beneficial it is to you to be following these patterns in your relationships. What would you like to change? Can you separate what happened to you as a child from what you need now as an adult? What small thing could you do differently that might break an unhealthy pattern in your relationships?

In this journal extract, Kevin explains what he learnt from doing this exercise:

When I explored my relationships I realized how much impact my family history was having on my choice of guys and my expectations. My dad died when I was seven and I believed that it was 'unsafe' to love anyone, because they would be taken away from me. I was choosing unsuitable and unavailable men, where the relationship never got close, so that I avoided the pain of being hurt. I realized I was just trading in one kind of pain for another. I was avoiding the pain of losing someone, but facing a different pain of never having a relationship that worked.

Only when I explored this in detail did I see how self-defeating my relationships were. I knew it would be hard, but I realized that I would have to consider finding a different kind of man and start to believe that if I truly loved someone and they left (or died), I would survive.

Now I am much more aware of what I look for in a guy. I am now at the early stages of a relationship with someone totally different from the usual arrogant and selfish types I fell for before! It is taking a lot of getting used to, and I'm not sure if I would call it 'love' yet, but I know I am moving towards something much more rewarding in the long run. (Kevin, theatre producer, 38)

By completing the above exercise I hope you will notice some of your own subconscious motives when looking for partners. The next stage is to decide, like Kevin, whether you need to try a different approach to relationships. It may not be easy or comfortable at first, but you will be finding ways to break out of any damaging cycles you perpetuate.

Looking for shoes in the shirt shop

Sukki was an interior designer, in her late thirties and very attractive, who had been through a painful divorce settlement five years before. There had been no children and Sukki desperately wanted a family before it was too late. When she came to see me, there had been a string of boyfriends in her life, but none seemed able to make a commitment to her. She was fed up and disillusioned. She felt that there must be something terribly wrong with her for each man, one after another, to treat her badly.

Her latest boyfriend, Piero, was a case in point. She met him at a nightclub. He was extremely good-looking and their sex life was adventurous, but he never included her in his social life and they only ever met at her flat. This repeated a pattern in common with other men in Sukki's life. Piero would not even give Sukki his home phone number. He made excuses so that they would never meet at his apartment and she started to feel anxious when she could not contact him, fearing that he was seeing other women. After a while, Sukki started to see herself merely as a sex object who was available at the beck and call of her boyfriend, but with whom there was no real love or intimacy. She was losing her self-respect and with it her self-esteem.

In her journal Sukki explored past relationships with men. She made a list of all her significant relationships and wrote a 'case history' of each one (see Exercise 3 in Chapter 2). She discovered that she always became involved with younger men she met at nightclubs and bars. When she was honest with herself, these men had in fact told her early on in the relationships that they were *not* looking for anything serious. She always hoped that by being with her and finding out how great that was, they would change their minds about this, but they never did. From the outset she was looking for a long-term relationship, while the men she became involved with were looking for something casual. Sukki realized that as long as she sought out these kinds of men – usually younger, very attractive and not ready to settle down – she would be disappointed.

It seemed clear that Sukki was looking for a man with commitment but was ending up with one man after another who was not able to offer this. I call this syndrome 'Looking for shoes in the shirt shop', where we look in the wrong place and therefore always find the wrong partners. When I explained this to Sukki, she was relieved to see that there was nothing 'wrong' with her, but that she was doing something which did not work, but which she could change.

Shortly after this point, Sukki went to a party for single people as part of a marketing promotion. While there, she met several men who were single fathers struggling to take care of a family, earn a living and have a social life. They shared her interest in family issues, which made her feel she had a common bond with these men (even though she had no children of her own), and with one, Julian, in particular.

Julian was slightly older than Sukki, with two children. His wife had died four years previously. He was not looking for a casual fling, but cautiously hoping to meet someone with whom he would eventually settle down to complete the family again. He was not the kind of man Sukki was usually attracted to, but she tentatively started to date him. They both wanted to take things slowly and as sincerely as possible. She was amazed to find that she experienced none of the difficulties she had found with her recent boyfriends. She felt respected and included in the whole of Julian's life. She did not feel a need to check up on him, because he was being open and honest with her, causing no blocks and requesting no conditions in their relationship. Her self-esteem had started to return, together with her sense of humour and zest for life.

Sukki has no idea whether things will work out in the long term with Julian, but at least she has started looking in the 'right place' for the sort of man with the qualities and intentions she truly wants.

Exercise 10: Are you looking in the right place?

Return to your notes on Exercise 3 in Chapter 2 and answer the following:

1 What patterns have you been repeating?

2 What kind of person have you been looking for?

3 Does that kind of person exist in the places where you are currently meeting people?

4 What changes might you need to make in order to meet someone suitable?

5 Where do you need to start looking for a more suitable person?

6 Where do you need to stop looking?

7 What qualities are you really looking for?

8 Do you need to look for different qualities in someone?

When it comes to an end

A successful relationship is not necessarily one that lasts. Indeed, a successful relationship could be one that was whole and complete in itself with all the right ingredients (such as love, honesty, trust, respect and equality), but which did not endure. Perhaps there is still fondness or a deep connection. This is not a failed relationship, but rather a good one that did not last a lifetime, for whatever reason.

Even when we are the one to end a relationship, it is easy for our self-esteem to suffer. It is understandable to feel a sense of doubt about the future and to acknowledge, even if you tried your hardest to help the relationship to work, that ultimately it did not survive. You might have a tendency, however, to view any relationship that is brought to an end deliberately as a 'failure'. Seeing it in this way can be a false and damaging conclusion, because you can tend to label yourself a failure too. There may well be great sadness, but you need to avoid jumping to the conclusion that you can 'never get it right'. Instead you can cherish fond memories and look after your feelings of loss without it meaning there is something wrong with you.

As a counsellor, I am often asked if former lovers can turn successfully into 'just good friends'. When we love someone and have created a strong bond with them, it is hard to let every part of that person go. It is tempting to want to hold on to as much of the connection as possible under another guise, especially if we are the injured party. My experience shows that it is possible, but there is a condition that generally helps and that condition involves the passage of time.

When people split up it is rare for both parties to shift into a new mode of being together, from lovers to friends, straight away. Unless the split is absolutely mutual (which it rarely is), usually one person will feel hurt and the other may well feel guilty, but 'free'. The injured party may have hidden hopes that by 'staying friends' their former partner will have a change of heart and want to return to being lovers. They may deny these motives even to themselves and be unable to let go and move on from the relationship. Under these circumstances, it is difficult for the friendship to work, because one person secretly wants it to be more than it is – they are hoping for change.

In my experience, the shift from lover to friend works best when there is a distinct break in contact over a period of time. Each person needs to be able to move on and perhaps begin a new relationship, before it is clear that only 'friendship' is the desired outcome. If one person cannot bear to see their ex-partner with another lover, then it is likely that they still harbour stronger feelings than friendship. Until these feelings subside, a true friendship is not possible, because more complicated emotions are getting in the way. Usually what's needed is a period of time when each person can experience life without the other at its centre.

6

Are we right for each other?

When love is not enough

It is important to recognize the role of compatibility in the likely success and endurance of any relationship. Couples who do not consider their differences and base their relationship purely on 'wanting to be together' can come across serious problems later on. Sadly, loving someone may not be enough if there is a mismatch in values, attitudes and life-plans between partners. When one partner has a vision for their life that the other does not aspire to, the relationship can falter, even when both partners sincerely love each other. This can mean that the partnership ends or that one person compromises to such an extent that resentment and long-term anger poison the relationship.

There needs to be a certain amount of overlap in priorities and lifestyles for individuals to follow their own path, and also be on the same map as their partner, heading roughly in the same direction. Take a look at the following diagrams.

Figure 5 shows the pie-charts that Jan and Bobby drew to show the relative weight and importance of certain factors in their lives. They were each asked to show how they valued the importance of: career, money, spirituality/religion, political views, travel, social life, having children and sex. You can see from the diagrams that there are very few similarities; in fact the only true match is with 'political views' (which reflects the fact that they met at a political rally). None of the other factors were viewed by Jan and Bobby with the same level of significance. Once they realized how different their underlying priorities in life were, Jan and Bobby could see why their relationship was struggling. They were devoted to each other, but the structures upon which their lives were built were too different to sustain a long-term partnership. Bobby wanted to travel and spread his wings, Jan wanted to settle and have children. Unfortunately their future together was doomed because of this fundamental lack of compatibility and before long they went their separate ways.

JAN

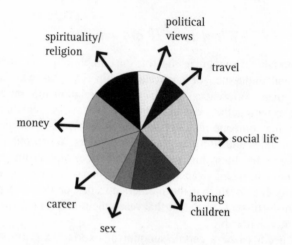

BOBBY

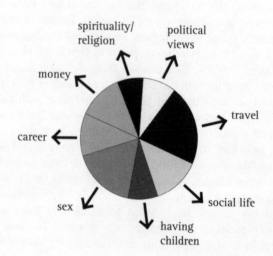

Figure 5: Measuring the important things in life

Compatibility check

Compatibility applies not only to *what* we do, but also to *how* we do it. Our attitude to money, for example, is crucial, especially at a stage in a relationship when couples are living together and own shared purchases. Someone who manages money well, who puts aside money into savings and never incurs debts will have a difficult time with someone who forgets to pay bills, does not save and regularly over-spends.

Pace of life and lifestyle also need to be considered. If one partner has lots of energy, gets up early, goes to bed late, likes to be out, busy rushing from one event to the other, they will find it hard to adjust to someone who has a slower and quieter pace of life. Our personality types come into play too. Some of us prefer to be spontaneous and impulsive, whereas others like to be organized and to plan ahead; some of us are energized by the buzz of constant activity, while others prefer solitude and time to reflect and recharge their batteries.

There are also differences of culture and social background to consider. Of course we are unlikely to be looking for someone who is a carbon copy of ourselves (probably too dull!), but we do need a degree of overlap or else the differences are too great to adjust to.

Exercise 11: Compatibility check

1 Consider the following areas and draw up a pie-chart (see Figure 5) to show how important each one is in your life. Alternatively rate each area on a scale of 1 to 10, where 1 is 'totally unimportant' and 10 is 'extremely important'.

career, money, spirituality/religion, political views, travel, social life, having children, sex

Add a few words to pinpoint why you have given your chosen ratings (for example, for 'career' you might put 'really important for me to reach the role of managing director by the time I am 30', or for 'money' you might add 'no burning ambition to have more possessions – happy with a simple lifestyle').

2 On a separate sheet you might also want to rate any interests you have, such as:

music, cinema, theatre, literature, art, sport and fitness, outdoor pursuits, spectator sports, games (including computer games), voluntary work, church, creative and artistic pursuits (drawing, writing, photography, DIY)

3 Also consider the following:

lifestyle, pace of life, work/life balance, role of your family (of origin), your vision for the future

4 In your answers to questions 1 to 3, put an asterisk beside those areas in which you believe it is essential for your partner to have a level of interest or view that *matches* yours. You might find, for example, that it is necessary for your partner to share your religious beliefs, whereas it is less essential that he or she shares any of your hobbies.

5 If you have a current partner, you might ask them to do this exercise for themselves so that you can compare ratings. Or you could complete this exercise as though from your partner's point of view and imagine how they would rate these factors. Even if you only do this exercise for yourself you will still have a useful blueprint showing the kinds of priorities you would like in common with a new partner.

6 If you have a current partner, make your own assessment based on your findings to judge how well suited you are in the important areas of life. Do your essential priorities match? Have you discussed your differences in any area? Do you need to address anything further? Couples often have most problems when their attitudes to money, having children and sex are incompatible.

Do not panic if on paper you seem to be poles apart from your partner. Knowing *how* to deal with areas of incompatibility can help considerably to bridge the gaps. Skills such as the ability to compromise and negotiate and qualities like acceptance, empathy and understanding are key in managing differences between you. Likewise, if you appear to be extremely well matched, these skills will still be useful in creating and sustaining harmony between you. The next exercise, on communication, should help you to develop these skills.

How well do you communicate?

We have more means of getting messages to each other in our current lifestyles than ever before. The telephone, mobile phone, fax, email (as well as traditional overland mail), online chat-rooms, phone-text and video-phone provide a multitude of ways of conveying information to each other. But how well are we understood by our nearest and dearest when we are with them face to face? How aware are we of the range of verbal communication skills and how well do we make use of them? This exercise will help you to assess how well you communicate. It can be carried out on your own or jointly with your partner. It could be the starting point for exploring the issues of compatibility described above, as well as any other issues between you.

Exercise 12: Rating your communication skills

We will examine five areas of communication: negotiating, listening and encouraging, attentiveness, expressing your feelings and verbal intimacy.

Consider the following areas of communication and rate yourself and your partner by putting a circle round the relevant words on the scale:

1 Negotiating

Negotiation between partners involves attempts to find solutions, decisions and compromises acceptable to both. It is the process whereby each person offers ideas to try to reach a conclusion to please both parties. It is a give-and-take process. When negotiating, you might be using words such as compromise, reconsider, discuss, agree, disagree, weigh up, consequences. For example, 'I don't wish to do what you suggest, but could we find a compromise between us?' or 'If you don't feel like going to Crete on holiday, where would you like to go and let's reconsider.' This sort of statement would then usually be followed by discussion between you.

How I rate my skills at negotiating:

POOR OCCASIONALLY GOOD USUALLY GOOD VERY GOOD EXCELLENT

How I rate my partner's skills at negotiating:

POOR OCCASIONALLY GOOD USUALLY GOOD VERY GOOD EXCELLENT

How I think my partner would rate *my* skills at negotiating:

POOR OCCASIONALLY GOOD USUALLY GOOD VERY GOOD EXCELLENT

If you have time, write down the reasons for rating this skill the way you did. For example, 'My skills at negotiating are "very good", because I try to be sensitive with my partner about any decisions that affect both of us.'

2 Listening and encouraging my partner to talk

This involves how helpful you are at giving your partner space to explore and discuss matters. You might be using phrases such as 'That's interesting, tell me more', or 'How do you feel about that?'

How I rate my skills at listening and encouraging my partner to talk:

POOR OCCASIONALLY GOOD USUALLY GOOD VERY GOOD EXCELLENT

How I rate my partner's skills at listening and encouraging me to talk:

POOR OCCASIONALLY GOOD USUALLY GOOD VERY GOOD EXCELLENT

How I think my partner would rate *my* ability to listen and to encourage her/him to talk:

POOR OCCASIONALLY GOOD USUALLY GOOD VERY GOOD EXCELLENT

Again add any examples which substantiate your reasons for your ratings.

3 Attentiveness

Attentiveness is the way you sense something intuitively about your partner, by noticing aspects of their behaviour and body language, without them having to tell you how they are feeling. It means taking the trouble to notice the signs and signals your partner is conveying. For example, 'You look really tired, do you want to stay in tonight?' or 'You seem very quiet, have I upset you?'

How I rate my attentiveness towards my partner:

POOR OCCASIONALLY GOOD USUALLY GOOD VERY GOOD EXCELLENT

How I rate my partner's attentiveness towards me:

POOR OCCASIONALLY GOOD USUALLY GOOD VERY GOOD EXCELLENT

How I think my partner would rate *my* attentiveness:

POOR OCCASIONALLY GOOD USUALLY GOOD VERY GOOD EXCELLENT

Add any examples which substantiate your reasons for your ratings.

4 Expressing what I am feeling

This refers to your ability to express your feelings about other people and situations through words and actions. You are likely to be using 'feeling' words such as upset, angry, sad, hurt, glad. For example, 'I think I might have hurt my mum by telling her I was too busy' or 'I am so glad about getting this letter from my cousin.'

How I rate my ability to express what I am feeling:

POOR OCCASIONALLY GOOD USUALLY GOOD VERY GOOD EXCELLENT

How I rate my partner's ability to express what she/he is feeling:

POOR OCCASIONALLY GOOD USUALLY GOOD VERY GOOD EXCELLENT

How I think my partner would rate *my* ability to express what I am feeling:

POOR OCCASIONALLY GOOD USUALLY GOOD VERY GOOD EXCELLENT

Add any examples which substantiate your reasons for your ratings.

5 Verbal intimacy

Verbal intimacy is slightly different from self-expression. Whereas 'expressing what I am feeling' (point 4 above) refers to 'talking about' your feelings about outside events or people, verbal intimacy involves expressing the immediate feelings you have towards your partner *to him or her directly*. This is usually more difficult, because it means saying what you feel frankly to your partner (rather than sharing your feelings with a third party).

You will be using 'feeling' words (similar to point 4) towards your partner, such as 'I feel frustrated with you because . . .' or 'I feel guilty every time you mention . . .' Verbal intimacy embraces negative as well as positive expression. For example, 'I feel inadequate when you tell me . . .' as well as 'I feel so warm inside when you say you love me.'

How I rate my verbal intimacy:

POOR OCCASIONALLY GOOD USUALLY GOOD VERY GOOD EXCELLENT

How I rate my partner's verbal intimacy:

POOR OCCASIONALLY GOOD USUALLY GOOD VERY GOOD EXCELLENT

How I think my partner would rate *my* verbal intimacy:

POOR OCCASIONALLY GOOD USUALLY GOOD VERY GOOD EXCELLENT

Add any examples which substantiate your reasons for your ratings.

You could also consider and rate other areas such as ability to trust, show understanding, empathy and respect, be sensitive, share humour, have fun, make decisions together and so on. Once your ratings are complete, review how well you judge yourself and your partner in each area of communication. You could also see whether your partner agrees with the rating you give yourself in each area.

This exercise is excellent for opening up communication between you! Use it to discuss each of your perceptions about what works well and which areas need improving. You can also imagine what you would each be doing differently if you were to move up on the rating scale by only one step. For example, under 'attentiveness' if you scored 'poor', you might decide that to reach 'occasionally good', you would need to take more trouble to notice your partner's body language in order to try to judge his or her mood better.

Styles of expressing love

Chapter 2 examined the role of our upbringing in determining our views of what love means to us. It is important also to understand the different ways in which individuals demonstrate love, as we each have our own natural preference.

Sandy explains how misunderstandings arose in her relationship due to different styles of expressing love:

> I was really keen on Pablo and felt that we had a lot going for us as a couple. But I always had this nagging doubt that he wasn't as committed as me, because he hardly ever said 'I love you'. I was always saying it to him and I started to feel insecure because I hardly ever heard it back. When I finally plucked up courage to ask him about it, he said that the way he showed his love was not through words, but by 'doing things' for me. He would cook me a special meal or get the weekly shop as a surprise – and to him, this was his way of expressing his love. I felt so relieved that he did feel the same way as me, but he just showed it differently! (Sandy, probation officer, 26)

We usually demonstrate our feelings of love using one or more of the following three ways:

- Verbal expression (such as by saying: 'I love you', 'You are wonderful' or 'I'm so happy when I'm with you').

- Physical expression (such as touching, holding, hugging, stroking or being sexual).
- Practical expression – doing something for the other person (such as booking a trip, organizing a treat or doing chores around the house).

You may realize instantly that you have a clear-cut preference for one of the above styles or that you, or your partner, feel most loved when all three styles are shown equally. Perhaps you need two approaches together, reinforcing each other, in order to get the full impact (such as your partner holding your hand as they show you something they have made for you that clearly took time and effort). The essential thing is to find out your individual preferences and then act on this, making sure that you include the style of loving preferred by your partner as far as possible.

If your preference for one or more of the above approaches does not seem obvious to you, think back in your current or previous relationships to moments when you have felt most cherished. When your partner has demonstrated love using the style that you prefer, you are likely to have felt an inner glow of deep contentment. If your partner has not got it right, you might have felt a sense of disappointment, as though something is lacking. Our self-esteem tends to suffer if we are not being offered the kind of love we need in the ways that feel most satisfying. We can feel like we are forever waiting for 'real' love to show itself. If this persists it can lead to feelings of loneliness and disillusion in the relationship, without us realizing that much of it could be down to a mismatch in the ways we are demonstrating our love.

When you feel sure you know your preferred way of receiving love, make sure your partner knows about and understands it, and vice versa. If there is disparity between you, you can then work out ways of fulfilling each other's needs. If, for example, your partner feels that you care most when you show physical expression (such as providing a back-rub), make sure you include this kind of activity on a regular basis. Making the effort to show love in the way your partner most prefers could make all the difference to your relationship.

Likewise, if your lover is not demonstrating love in your chosen way, explain what he or she needs to do, or say, to get it right. An effective way to do this is to remind your partner about a situation from your history together when their approach towards you had the desired effect. Something like: 'Do you remember the time when we didn't have much money and you took the trouble to build me a display case for Christmas – I appreciate it when you do thoughtful things like that for me . . .'

When styles of expressing love differ

If you realize that your favoured style of loving is different from your partner's, there is no need to be concerned. What matters is that you recognize your individual preferences and, if they are different, you work out ways of making sure each of you feels genuinely and deeply loved. If your partner's style of loving is different from your own, you may need to make an extra effort to show love in the way they experience it most sincerely in order to prevent misinterpretations. Insecurities and doubts about the levels of love shown in a relationship can often be immediately resolved by understanding the different ways love can be expressed.

The balance of power

The impact of unequal self-esteem between partners was mentioned in Chapter 1. 'Power' is another factor affecting the balance between partners. This section will help you assess the power dynamic in your relationship – what it means and what the consequences are. You will be asking yourself questions such as: 'Who is pulling the strings in my relationship?' 'Who leads and who follows?' 'Who fits in with the other person?' 'Who has the final say?'

Assessing power in this context means looking at not only who tends to have more self-esteem, but also who has more status, more control and even more money in the relationship. Life-events, such as a bereavement or job-loss can radically alter the balance of power between partners. Steve and Denise experienced this in their relationship. Steve was a managing director when severe job cuts were announced. He was used to being the main breadwinner in the family and Denise was happy for him to have more responsibility and more say. When Steve lost his job, he also lost his confidence and became withdrawn and depressed. Denise encouraged and supported him during this period and became the more powerful partner for a while. The balance of power had therefore swung from one partner to the other and this is normal as life-events take their toll on all of us.

Problems arise when the dynamic in the relationship does not allow the balance of power to swing back and forth. There will be times when one partner is feeling ill or vulnerable and they need more support; at other times they will need to be the stronger party and the one to offer encouragement. If the balance is always tipped in favour of one partner to the detriment of the other, then the whole relationship is out of balance and is likely to suffer.

For relationships to work well each person needs to feel they are able to both take the lead at times *and* take a back seat according to circumstances. David's story illustrates this:

> *I was struggling to find work after my car accident and Gina was brilliant at the time, taking care of me, as well as working extra shifts at the hospital. I was still in a lot of pain and found it hard to manage normal activities. Six months later, though, Gina had a miscarriage and our roles were reversed. I did more hours at work (I'd managed to get a teaching job) and I was there for her at a time when she couldn't cope. (David, secondary teacher, 30)*

David's story shows how he and his partner could depend on each other and allow the power to pass back and forth between them. It meant that as a couple they could cope with the many twists and turns that life held in store for them. Danielle explains, however, what happens when this does not work so well:

> *Pete was always the 'leader' in our marriage – he was confident and capable and I was happy to let him have this role. After his father died things got tense between us. I tried to be supportive and to help him to talk about his feelings, but he stone-walled me. He couldn't bear to let anyone see he was suffering, and he wouldn't accept anything from me and pushed me away. I felt so distant from him that in the end I have to admit I had an affair. We broke up shortly afterwards. (Danielle, front of house manager, 36)*

In Danielle and Pete's case there was a fixed imbalance of power. Pete refused to allow Danielle to support him at his time of need. She in turn felt her efforts were being rejected and felt hurt. Ultimately, Danielle felt Pete did not need what she had to offer and she began to look elsewhere for a more fulfilling relationship.

Exercise 13: The power inventory

1 Take a look at the following list of life changes:

Job:	job change, promotion, demotion, redundancy, being fired
Family/Friends:	illness of relatives or close friends, bereavement, suicide
Sex:	infidelity, impotence, loss of libido, sexually transmitted disease
Having children:	a new birth, termination, miscarriage, loss of a child, infertility
Health:	accident, illness, disability, weight loss or gain
Other:	moving house, children leaving home, sudden loss of income (for example, due to the stock market), sudden increase in income (such as a legacy)

2 Consider whether your relationship has been through any of these changes.

3 If so, how did the change affect the balance of power between you? Did you take on more power or less power as a result of the change? What impact did this have on you? What impact did this have on your partner?

4 Are you able to pass power back and forth between you in the relationship according to outside events? Can you take the lead and support your partner when needed? Can your partner do this for you when you need it? Can you receive support? Can your partner?

5 Can you see a way whereby the power dynamic could work better for your relationship? As a result of your discoveries you may need to discuss the dynamic of power with your partner.

Rather like a see-saw, healthy partnerships allow each person to be in turn the strong one and the more needy one, and as long as it can shift both ways this flexibility can work well to cover most eventualities. This kind of equality is not something fixed, whereby both parties need to have the *same* income or make the *same* contribution; rather it is the ability to share reciprocal roles and that this is given credit and accepted by each person. It shows that together you are a true team.

Respect

Love is composed of many qualities, and alongside honesty, trust and equality, 'respect' plays a significant part. Without respect it is hard for any relationship to survive. A lack of respect can damage our self-esteem. If, for example, your partner is bullying you, making fun of you or not taking your views seriously, your self-esteem is likely to suffer as a result.

Exercise 14: **The respect inventory**

1 How much do you feel respected by your partner in the following areas:

your job or role, your appearance, your intelligence, your abilities, your habits, your friends, your interests and leisure pursuits, your parents and family, your background, your religious or spiritual views, your opinions, your political views

2 Are there any areas where you do not feel respected by your partner? If so, how will you address this?

3 Considering the subjects in question 1 again, how respectful do you think you are towards your partner in these areas? Are there any areas where you and your partner could improve your respect towards each other?

Respect is not about agreeing with your partner's opinion or decisions, but rather about both of you honouring and accepting as far as is possible all the different facets that make up who you are. When you disagree with a view or choice made by your partner, you can learn to put forward your case in a respectful way, stating how you feel about it, rather than disparaging it (you can see more about this in the section on assertiveness in Chapter 10). If you are vegetarian, for example, and your partner eats meat, you will need to be respectful around each other. You may need to draw up boundaries in the kitchen (such as keeping chopping boards separate) so that both of your standpoints about food can live side by side.

If there is something that you cannot tolerate at all in your partner, you will need to work out how you will deal with it together. For example, if you cannot bear cigarette smoke and you live with a heavy smoker, you will need to discuss this diplomatically, to show respect, and to discuss boundaries and acceptable 'rules' around smoking in your home. In this way, even factors that you dislike about each other can be incorporated into a healthy relationship and need not become the cause of unnecessary rifts between you.

7

Trying to be someone else

For many years I was dissatisfied with my personality. I felt that I 'should' be more outgoing, more sociable and more entertaining. Many times I tried to be this new person, putting on a mask and grappling with it to make it fit. My true nature, however, is more reserved and introspective. I genuinely prefer my own company, or intimate discussions, to bustling parties. Nevertheless, I used to marvel at the way other people could be quick-witted and amusing and I wanted to be like that.

There is a difference now. I still get tongue-tied, especially when encountering someone with an overbearing personality, but I am able to accept myself. I no longer feel second-rate nor do I feel I need to apologize for being introverted. I am no longer hiding my real nature with a mask. By learning to accept and respect my own nature, I see that other people accept the way I am too. The irony is that when I accept myself and relax, there are times when I can be the life and soul of the party after all.

The masks you wear

Unfortunately, many of us have trapped ourselves into trying to be somebody we are not. We fear that being ourselves is 'not enough' and this is where our need for a mask begins. We do not like certain aspects of ourselves, so we hide these qualities (or 'faults' as we might critically describe them). We try to disguise our true natures and bluff our way through situations. Some of the behaviours we try to emulate never suited us in the first place. (I tried, for example, to be funny and entertaining, when my best quality is to be a good listener.) We go about our lives wearing masks that do not fit and then get trapped, because we have established a false image that everyone expects us to maintain. Sadly, it means that our true self is squashed and unappreciated, particularly by ourselves, and this can often lead to anger, resentment, guilt, shame, bitterness and even depression.

The masked or false self often arises out of a need for approval and fear of rejection. Jackson was someone who had been presenting a false self to the world for most of his life:

I hate conflict, so I have always tried to smooth things over, even as a kid. I've always tried to make things right for other people and I put my own needs to one side. I took the subjects at college that my father wanted me to do and ended up in a career I had no real interest in, but which kept everyone else happy. In my marriage, I was always the first to give in, agreeing to things I didn't want, just to keep the peace. (Jackson, former computer programmer, 33)

Jackson eventually had a nervous breakdown, because he could no longer carry on pretending. He hated his computer work, he was not sure whether he loved his wife and he did not know *who he was* any more, because he had spent so many years denying his own true nature.

How did he break this cycle? How did he learn to accept and value himself? Through using his journal and through our counselling work together, Jackson started to get a feel for the activities that truly ignited his energy. He looked back in his life to find times when he really liked himself. He started to re-evaluate everything in his life from the point of view of his 'heart' rather than his 'head'. He identified and challenged many beliefs he held which consisted of 'shoulds' and 'oughts' and pressures he had taken on from other people. Jackson saw how much of his lifestyle was governed by what he thought other people wanted.

After several months, Jackson started to undertake activities he wanted to do, but had denied himself because of his drive to please others. He began music lessons again (he had given them up in his teens to concentrate on 'serious' study). He also began to sketch and paint. I was fascinated to see a new creative person emerging from the repressed one I had met months earlier. Jackson became relaxed, more easygoing and his sense of humour returned. He no longer felt trapped and he could identify more choices for himself. Ultimately, his breakdown had become a breakthrough into a way of being which truly belonged to him and which his old self could no longer sustain. He had started to peel away the masks.

With time, Jackson made a complete career change. Also, after much soul-searching, but with a greater understanding of his needs, he decided to leave his wife. Despite the pain, loss and uncertainty, he climbed out of his black hole, leaving his false self behind him, taking forward a new enthusiasm and motivation. He now has hopes for a future based on an expansion of his genuine, not fabricated, self and aims to develop new relationships that he really believes in.

Exercise 15: Who are you?

Try answering the questions below in your journal in order to gain a deeper sense of yourself:

1 How would your life be different if you were wholeheartedly being your true self?

2 If you were to be 100 per cent your true self in work, in relationships and with family, friends and strangers, who would you be? Try describing a typical day, if you were to be your genuine self with no reservations. If you describe something that is poles apart from the kind of day you normally have, then this tells you how removed you are from your genuine self.

3 With whom are you most able to be yourself? When do you like yourself most? Which kinds of people help you to relax and which kinds of people cause you to be on your guard? What does this tell you about yourself?

4 What are your priorities? List them. What is most important to you at this moment in your life? (Perhaps it is building a loving relationship, or having an exciting social life, enjoying a secure family, financial reward, achieving, having adventures, climbing the status ladder, being fulfilled in your work, taking care of your health, taking part in leisure pursuits and hobbies, helping other people, making a difference in the world.)

5 Look at your answer to question 4. Are the priorities you listed your own? Are you working towards priorities you think you 'ought' to have? Are you working towards priorities you associate with your father, mother, family or society in general?

6 Are you where you want to be in life? Whose life are you living? Are you living from your head (what you think you 'should' do) or from your heart (what you truly desire)?

The above questions will help you to see how much you are

following your own unique path in life and how much you may have been pulled off course by the expectations of others. You may realize that you have lost touch with your own personal vision, interests and abilities in order to try to do what you think is expected of you. Many ideas in this book will help you towards reclaiming your individuality and building a life that truly reflects the person you are.

If I am more myself, won't I become selfish?

Jackson feared that friends, family or colleagues at work would not accept him if he showed certain aspects of his true self. Being your real self does not mean being ruthlessly selfish. It does not mean abandoning all social codes and appropriate behaviour. We can be ourselves and be honest while also being sensitive to others. By basing our interactions on equality and mutual respect, we can state what we feel or want clearly and politely, and be willing to respectfully receive honesty from others. We will then start to stand up for ourselves while also valuing the other person's position.

Shaking off your false self and emerging as your real self takes time and a great deal of self-awareness and courage. You will need to peel away the layers of your feelings, actions and behaviours and find out how genuine they are for you. Are you hiding aspects of your real self away? Is the person people see the true you or an act? Do you pretend you do not feel certain emotions?

The foundation is to rediscover your true emotions. You may have been putting a lid on certain emotions, such as anger, sadness or grief, because they have felt unacceptable, or people would be shocked to see you expressing them.

Approval-seeking

One of the hallmark behaviours of low self-esteem is the tendency to try to please other people to the detriment of our own needs and wishes. Approval-seeking is an outward expression of a passive approach (see 'Four Styles of Behaviour' in Chapter 10). We might assume that if we say and do things to put someone else first, we will be liked or loved by that person. However, this behaviour has a number of flaws and in the long run is likely to backfire.

A simple example of approval-seeking is when we respond to a question such as 'Which film would you like to see at the cinema?' with 'I don't mind', 'Whatever you like' or 'You choose'. This might seem as though we are being flexible and kind, but it also passes the onus back to the other person. They then have to take responsibility for the choice of film, instead of sharing it with us. If this approval-seeking behaviour persists, it can backfire. It can be *annoying* for the other person to have no ideas or feedback from us and they can become tired of our lack of initiative or our inability to make decisions.

Take a look at the following:

The pitfalls of trying to please

- We may think that we are doing something to suit someone else, when in fact we have got it wrong. It may not be what they want. They may be silently frustrated or irritated with us.
- We may be doing something that the other person *does* want from us, but they may secretly feel contempt towards us for having such little self-respect.
- We may be doing something the other person wants, but they take it for granted, hardly notice it and keep expecting similar treatment or responses.
- We may be doing something the other person wants and they may give us 'love on approval' for it. In other words, as long as we are being this way, they will like us, but not if we stop. Then we are forced to keep on doing what they want for ever in order to maintain this so-called love.
- By pleasing others, our true feelings and desires are dismissed and ignored. If our feelings are repressed, they still exist as energy within us. They may take on a destructive force of their own, such as resentment, depression or uncontrollable anger, or even as illness and disease.

The value of anger

In Chapter 10 we examine assertiveness as a valuable tool in expressing equality, honesty and respect. When you begin your work on assertiveness, you may be afraid that by standing up for yourself and expressing what you feel you will become too aggressive. This is a common misconception and people often confuse anger with hostility, when they are not the same thing. Assertive-anger does not mean throwing a tantrum in order to get your message across; it is about finding a way of saying 'What you did is not acceptable'. Assertive-anger will usually give the other person choices (such as how to go about rectifying a problem), whereas aggressive-anger can feel like an attack and in its most extreme form can even turn into violence.

Anger is an energy which, when used assertively and not aggressively, can help towards resolving difficult situations. In this way it is a powerful agent for getting things that seem unfair to you changed, and it can therefore be positive and valuable. When others know you are angry, they are invited to reconsider their behaviours or rules. The alternative is for you to hide your anger and silently complain to yourself, so that the source of the problem is never challenged.

Dealing with our anger

Of course, there will be times when you feel anger and it does not seem appropriate or beneficial to express that anger straight away. This is where your self-awareness can help you. You can notice what you are feeling, acknowledge and respect the feeling within yourself and then return to your anger later on, at a time when you can give full and fair vent to it. One aspect of self-esteem is to encourage and value our feelings and to look after ourselves when we have them. If someone has upset you just before you need to deal with a completely different situation, promise yourself that you will return to the anger you felt and process it. Your journal will be a useful tool at such times, allowing you to express and explore the feelings in full. When the anger is too overwhelming for writing, you could thump pillows, go for a walk and scream and rant in a place of solitude or do some vigorous exercise to expel the energy. Later you can use your journal to reflect on the situation.

Anger often consists of either 'fear' or 'hurt'. Imagine a scenario when a car-driver nearly knocks over a pedestrian. Both parties usually react by getting angry, expressing their fear at the sudden near miss. Imagine another scenario, when someone finds out that their partner is having an affair. The anger expressed by the injured party is mostly hurt; it is saying 'I can't believe it – I thought you loved me; now I feel utterly rejected.'

Whenever you next experience anger take a moment to ask

yourself what your anger is really saying. Ask yourself whether it is about fear or hurt (or maybe both). This might help you to understand and deal with your anger better.

In the next chapter we look at how the fear of rejection can get in the way of being ourselves.

8

Daring to be yourself

The fear of rejection

The fear of being rejected is one of the biggest blocks to getting romantically involved with someone. Sometimes the fear is so great that we never risk getting into a relationship in the first place – or we create barriers to prevent one from developing. Alternatively, we might worry that if we dare to reveal our true self, we will only be rejected, so we play the part of somebody else. Feelings of inadequacy may lead us to try to present an image that seems 'better', more loveable and more attractive to the person we are trying to impress.

Once in a relationship this fear of rejection can continue. When we are not sure about the other person's level of commitment, we may not be prepared to take the risk of revealing anything complicated. If we feel we are being mistreated, for example, we may try to ignore this or find excuses for it. We do not want to put pressure on the relationship, because we do not know if the relationship can sustain it. So we avoid rocking the boat and the problem-issues remain undisclosed, the real feelings and behaviours stay hidden. Nothing is dealt with, but at least we keep the relationship on an even keel for the time being.

The fear of rejection, or the fear of being alone, often persuades us to remain in our current relationship, even though we may be unhappy. Take a look at these two scenarios:

Jackie told me how she had pretended to be more outgoing than she really was for nearly a year with her latest boyfriend, Steve. She was very keen on him, but she felt that her true self would be too boring for him, so she made up a false bubbly persona to try to keep him interested. Steve asked her to move in with him and she was ecstatic – at last she had secured her man. Sadly, things went wrong after that. She no longer had her own space to be her natural reflective self and tried to keep up the front of being the live wire all the time. She became stressed and anxious as she continued to play this part to Steve, who was becoming increasingly confused by her Jekyll and Hyde mood swings. Eventually Jackie knew she could not carry on pretending. She was unhappy and finally she ended the relationship.

Rik could not work out why his relationships did not last. He was 35 and had had only one relationship that lasted longer than a few months. Rik always played the role of Mr Wonderful when he was courting a woman to impress her and make her want him. He went out of his way to please his girlfriends: sending them flowers, lavishing expensive meals on them, helping out with DIY. The women in his life were initially bowled over by his approach and felt special. After a few months, however, they become bored with him. He seemed to have no real substance or opinions and came across as too eager to please. Women usually finished the relationship with him after a few months and Rik failed to understand what the problem was.

Each of the two cases has the same theme. The fear of rejection caused both Jackie and Rik to present a false self, but in the long run this led to their downfall.

The drawbacks in presenting a false self

Both Jackie and Rik were trying to be something they were not and were missing out because of it. They were caught up in a pattern of not being authentic in relationships, because they thought it would work better that way. Each false self created an untenable situation that eventually collapsed.

Jackie and Rik presented their masks right from the start, hoping this self would be more attractive. Jackie realized that the longer she stayed in the relationship, the harder it became to pretend to be who she was not. Her real self did not have room to breathe, and hidden resentment, anger and frustration began to brew. Rik was trying too hard to be what he thought women want. He could not see that his girlfriends felt smothered and wanted to see more of his real personality without all the gifts.

Avoiding risks

In the cases above, the protagonists were not prepared to take the risk to see if the relationships were strong enough to rise above the difficulties. Jackie was afraid to show her quiet side, Rik was afraid to let go of playing the 'ideal man'. The irony is that each relationship failed and subsequent ones will probably do so too, unless these patterns are challenged.

Your 'best' self versus your 'false' self

At the beginning of a new relationship it is understandable that we want to make a good impression. We need to be careful, however, that we present our 'best' self and not a 'false' self. There could have been two different outcomes if everyone in the above scenarios had dared to be themselves. Of course, the relationships may still have come to an end, but the chances of success could have been higher, due to greater levels of honesty.

Jackie could have been her real self – quiet, modest and reserved. Steve might indeed have found this behaviour dull, in which case he would not have been the most suitable personality for Jackie in the first place. But Steve might also have found her fascinating for her depth and intellect.

Rik could have been himself from the start, showing his natural generosity and kindness at times, but without this being the focus of the relationship. He could have been more natural and allowed his personality to shine through. The chances are that at some point he would have met someone with whom he found a level of compatibility, without having to try so hard all the time.

Daring to be ourselves means learning to be true to our own personalities and honest about our views and feelings. Only when we allow ourselves to be honest can we build emotional intimacy that forms the backbone of strong relationships.

What is emotional intimacy?

When we use the word 'intimacy' many of us think first of physical closeness and sex. Emotional intimacy, however, is the sharing of our deepest thoughts and feelings with someone within the context of honesty and trust. It is the sharing of honest feelings that brings people together. When we bare our soul to someone we are showing that we trust him or her and can be vulnerable with them. This in turn can lead to the other person feeling valued and special.

Can you recall a time when someone told you in confidence something about which they felt ashamed or hurt? Do you remember how you felt? Usually we feel touched and privileged to think that someone is able to confide in and trust us in this way. It makes us in turn want to share our fears and difficulties with them. It creates a safe place in which to bring our emotions. One of the most difficult forms of honesty is facing someone with the feelings that you have *about them*, yet this can lead to a greater depth of intimacy between two people, whether in a romantic relationship or a close friendship. (This is discussed in the section on communication skills in Chapter 6.)

When Graham dared to share the anger he felt towards his girlfriend, he had a surprisingly positive response:

I finally told my girlfriend how angry I was at the way she always ignored me when her friends were on the scene. For weeks I had harboured a grudge about it, but not said anything. Debbie was shocked at seeing me angry towards her, but then she said she was relieved to be able to talk about it. She explained how difficult it was to be with me and all her old friends together in one place, and she didn't know how to behave. We then had our very first heart-to-heart and talked honestly about our relationship. (Graham, store supervisor, 28)

It would be misleading to suggest that everyone should or will respond in this positive way when we are honest, but if we build people we can trust into our lives, there is more chance that they will offer this kind of understanding. When important things are left unsaid, it can cause a distance between two people, until the air is cleared between them. I remember uncertainty about my feelings towards my partner (who later became my husband), which created a distance in the early days of our relationship. On one occasion when we met up, it felt like there was something heavy and unspoken that was spoiling the way we interacted. I gradually plucked up the courage to mention my doubts about him and he was completely accepting of my feelings. He said he thought my doubts were normal and was not offended or upset. The result was that I felt relieved, my doubts instantly grew smaller and our subsequent discussion brought us closer together.

Exercise 16: Can you dare to be honest?

How different would your relationship be if you dared to be more honest?

- Try, for one week, being as honest as you can be with your partner.
- Try to avoid 'white lies', playing things down and not owning up.
- Find the right time to share something that feels daunting or awkward with your partner.
- Try to be considerate and diplomatic, especially if you are explaining something that might upset your partner.
- Use 'I feel . . .' statements when sharing emotional intimacy.
- Remember that it is hard to be genuinely honest if you are not in touch with your own feelings. Give yourself time, before you talk to your partner about emotional issues, to dig deep within yourself to find out how you feel. The 'agony aunt' method in my book *The Self-Esteem Journal* should give you some help in identifying feelings you may not know you have.
- Remember that 'bottling things up' and hiding your true feelings can lead to resentment and can poison a relationship.

It can be extremely scary to dare to reveal certain feelings and to be truly 'known'. Yet, ironically, ultimately being seen, known, understood and still being loved regardless is what we probably want most of all. Mutual honesty paves the way for deeper and braver encounters with people and the rewards for this are close, intimate relationships.

It is worth remembering that relationships (especially in their later years) can survive without sex, but rarely survive without emotional intimacy.

Coping with rejection

The sad fact about life is that no one can get through it without being rejected at some time. I cannot name anyone I know, including myself, who has not had to face some kind of painful rejection in their lives. Rejection will always be distressing. We have to face this and carry on knowing that it is unavoidable. We can be prepared to cope with rejection, build up a tolerance for it, and be ready to take it on and emerge stronger, having learnt something from the experience.

Exercise 17: How to cope with rejection

Listed below are some ideas to help you feel less crushed by rejection:

1 Build up a tolerance for rejection, so that it does not destroy your self-esteem when a break-up happens. This tolerance depends on how we view the break-up and how we view ourselves. Seeing the other person as 'missing out' by not choosing to stay with you is a positive way to view this, rather than focusing on your inadequacies. Remember what others (such as long-term friends) like about you and let them remind you about all your positive qualities, as this can help to restore your self-esteem.

2 Be careful with the language you use in describing how a relationship ended. Saying 'We split up, but I'm learning to be more honest' is more positive than saying 'I failed again'. Splitting up will always be painful, but we often forget the great feeling of relief when a relationship that has been causing us distress comes to an end.

3 Know that you will survive if the worst happens. Remember to keep a balance in your life so that your relationship does not become the be-all and end-all of your existence. If your relationship breaks down, you will still have all the other important elements of your life (such as work, friends, interests, family and so on).

4 Remember that lots of factors need to be compatible for a relationship to work and that loving each other may not always be enough. The most common difficulties that arise in relationships are related to money, having children and how couples see their futures. Even when couples believe they truly love each other, the relationship can break down because of these incompatibilities (see Chapter 6).

Daring to be yourself

Being as truly ourselves as possible is a consistent foundation, from which we can learn more easily if things go wrong. If we are trying to be different people from one relationship to the next, trying to fit in with the particular needs and interests of each partner, it will be hard for us to see what we do well in relationships and to build on our strengths.

Exercise 18: How to dare to be yourself

Here are some hints and areas to explore to help you to avoid the unfortunate scenarios of Jackie and Rik:

1 Notice when you are presenting a false self in relationships. Use your journal to reflect on the following:

- Are you being your true self with your current partner?
- Are you trying to act in a certain way merely to keep the relationship going?
- Are you so eager to please that you have lost sight of who your true self is?
- Are you denying certain important aspects of yourself?
- Are you trying to convince yourself that everything is fine in the relationship, when underneath you are putting up with things that do not feel right?

2 It is easier to notice what went wrong in a relationship well after the event itself and much harder to recognize what is going on at the time. Look back to earlier significant relationships and ask yourself the questions above, with regard to those relationships.

3 Try not to blame and berate yourself if you notice patterns emerging where you have not been honest in the past. Just know that you are now aware of these patterns and make a commitment to yourself to learn from them.

Once we notice that we have been putting on a mask, a brave face or trying to be a person we are not, we have a choice either to continue as we have been, or to risk making some changes.

Before we launch into the nature of those changes, let's use the next chapter to take stock of your support network and platonic friendships, as the changes you might wish to make will affect these too.

9

A closer look at friendships

In this chapter we look further than your main romantic relationship to consider the broader impact of friendships in your life. Friendships are often the backbone of our support network (including some family members) and provide us with a place to take our concerns as well as to share fun and joyful experiences. It is important to review the role and significance of these friends to check that your support network is as strong as it needs to be. Furthermore, good friends can sometimes evolve into long-term romantic relationships, so if you are currently without a partner, you may need to look no further than your current circle of friends to find that special someone!

Exercise 19: Drawing your support network

This exercise helps you to look at your friendships from a new angle by drawing the images you associate with them and then labelling what each person means to you.

1 Start with some crayons and a blank sheet of paper. Write down the names of everyone in your current support network. These are people you can turn to and trust with your innermost thoughts and feelings.

2 Draw the outline of a flower shape, with a 'petal' to represent each friend. Inside the individual petals, write the name or initials of each friend.

3 Close your eyes and as you reflect on each friend, allow an image to emerge that conjures up the essence of that person for you. Draw the image inside each petal beside their names.

4 Think also of the qualities that this friend gives you; perhaps you feel particularly 'connected' to this friend or feel 'warmth' or 'trust' when you think of them. Notice any negative factors or anything that is missing from the friendship as well as the positive aspects. Add all these words alongside each petal until you have filled out all the details of your support system.

You should now have a clearer sense of the role of each person in your life – what it is they offer you, their special qualities. If there are negative aspects, you might want to think of ways of addressing those issues. For example, if someone in your life is often unreliable or lets you down, you might want to explore this with that person. Explain how you feel about this and give them a chance to explain. Let them know what you *appreciate* about them also. This can help you to see the unique characteristics of each friend and perhaps where the gaps are too. For example, you might have lots of friends you have fun with, but very few you can be emotionally close with. Or perhaps you have friends who predominantly tell you their problems, but few who seem to have time to hear yours.

Drained or energized?

You may also find it helpful to consider the people who leave you feeling energized and those who seem to deplete your reserves and leave you feeling drained. Perhaps you have a friend who is over-demanding, or one who seems angry and negative most of the time. The following exercise allows you to see how close you are to each friend and whether you want to make any changes to the friendships you have.

Exercise 20: Drawing your circle of friends

1 On a sheet of paper, draw a series of circles around each other, starting with one in the centre about the size of a five-pence piece. Draw larger ones around this, leaving spaces of about one centimetre between the circles, until you reach the edge of the page. You will probably have about six circles looking like a target.

2 Inside the smallest circle in the middle put 'Me' or your own name. Then consider those friends who are closest to you. They may not necessarily be the ones you see most often, but they will be the friend or friends who you feel most comfortable with, who you can bare your soul to, or whose company you enjoy the most. Add their names to the circle adjacent to the smallest central one.

3 Then consider who you might place in the next band of friendship. These will be people you have a lot in common with, but perhaps do not know as well as those in the closest band, or do not find so interesting or comfortable. Add their names to this band.

4 Carry on until you have placed names in each band on the page. Leave a band empty if you feel that there is no friend who fits into it. For example, if you feel that there is no one who you feel extremely close to right now, you might leave the band adjacent to your own name blank.

5 Add the names of any acquaintances, work colleagues and new people you have met, but do not know well enough yet to consider 'friends', to the space outside the largest circle.

6 Once you have given everyone a position on your page, look at each one individually and ask yourself the following: 'Within my circle of friends, is this person getting closer to me?'

Maybe a friend has recently become closer to you following some kind of crisis. Perhaps you have only just started to get to know this person and you have a positive feeling about the rapport you have established. If it feels like the person is moving closer to you, put an arrow pointing *inwards* adjacent to their name. Let the arrow lead to the new place on your diagram where you would like them to be (see Figure 6).

7 Then ask yourself the opposite: 'Within my circle of friends, is this person moving further away?'

Perhaps a friend has left the region where you live and you do not see them so regularly, resulting in a feeling of estrangement between you. Maybe you feel that this friend has let you down. If you feel that the person is moving further away, add an arrow pointing *outwards* on the circle to the place where you now think they should be (this may be one or more adjacent circles further out) or where you feel this relationship may now be heading.

8 If you feel that a relationship has not gone through any changes recently, nor would you wish to move that friend on your circle, then add no arrows.

9 You will now see a picture emerging of how your circle of friends is changing. Some of the changes might be caused by outside circumstances, such as a friend who has just had a child and now has less time to see you, or another who has recently moved to the same location. Other changes may be those you wish to bring about

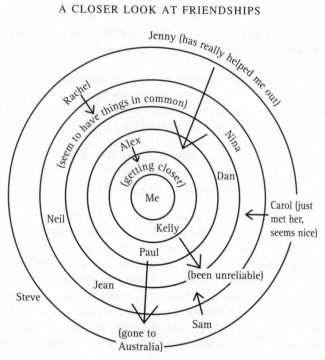

Figure 6: Your circle of friends

deliberately, either because you wish to make more of a friendship or because you wish to reduce contact in one that is not working so well any more.

10 Consider the friends who have arrows pointing inwards. These are the friendships that you feel are developing. What will you do on a practical level to ensure that these friends take their places in an inner band on your circle? How can you 'bring in' these friends so they become closer? This might involve invitations to spend more time together or suggestions about holidays, trips or events to share. Or it could mean simple messages of friendship and support sent in cards or on email.

11 Consider the friends who have arrows pointing outwards. These are the friends with whom you are reducing contact or letting go. Do you need to settle any outstanding issues with any of these people? Do you need to let them know that your paths are moving further apart? Are you drifting in different directions so much that you need to let go of them altogether? How will you address this? You may wish to send a letter explaining your feelings or suggest you meet face to face to say a proper goodbye.

This is a powerful exercise for helping you to see where you stand with the people in your life who you call 'friends'. It can help you to see that friendships fluctuate and that sometimes our relationships need an evaluation of this sort to see if they are still serving all concerned. As a result of this exercise you may find that you need to move on and leave some friends behind. This is especially so if you are becoming more assertive and clearer about which influences are positive to have around and which are not. This can be a sad recognition, but it then leaves space for new friends who are more suitable for you. Conversely, you may realize that you have a number of potential friends waiting in the wings, who you can now actively invite into your life to play a more prominent role.

The six questions

The following exercise can be daunting, but also powerful and positive if you dare to do it.

Exercise 21: Six questions to ask close friends

1 Select in your mind four or five of your most supportive friends (including your partner if you have one, or any close member of your family). Put yourself in their shoes and imagine how they would answer the following six questions about you. On a sheet of paper, put down your speculations about these people's responses.

- When you first met me, what was your first impression?
- Now you know me, how has your first impression changed?
- What do you think is the most interesting or appealing thing about me?
- What do you think are my most natural abilities?
- What do you think are my greatest strengths?
- What do you appreciate most about our friendship/relationship?

2 Once you have noted what you imagine others would say, approach these same people and find out what their *actual* responses are. If it would be more comfortable for you, you might like to post or email the questions so that you give them time to think and avoid embarrassment.

3 Compare your own answers with the ones you received from others. Then answer the following:

- Were you surprised by any of the responses you received?
- What themes were there?
- What are people's general opinions of you?
- Did your perceptions of yourself match the ones you received from your friends?
- What aspects of your personality are you under-valuing?

While this exercise needs some courage to complete, it can be rewarding and give your self-esteem a boost. Often we fail to acknowledge in ourselves the very qualities our friends love us for. Remember too that this exercise will tell you a lot about the individuals who completed it for you. Their answers will reflect their own values and what they believe are the important attributes in a friend. In turn you can offer to answer the same questions for these friends to help their own personal development and to show your appreciation of them.

A letter of support

This exercise is designed to help you to focus on recognizing and appreciating all the qualities and characteristics that make up who you are.

Exercise 22: Writing your letter of support

1 Think of someone from either your past or your present who has shown their support of you in some way – a former teacher who encouraged you to pursue a gift for drawing, say, or a family member who took you under their wing when your parents went through a bad

78

patch. It needs to be someone who showed complete faith in you, who did not judge you or have expectations of you. If you cannot think of anyone, imagine someone who might show these supportive traits. It could be a character from a film, a book or even a cartoon figure. If you are religious or spiritual, you might choose an angel or saint. Imagine this character is someone to whom you are going to write a letter stating your current situation in life.

2 Write a letter to the 'person' you have chosen. (You will not be sending it, so don't worry about their address!) Tell this person about your life, your feelings, your plans, your hopes – open your heart and imagine this person's kind and loving attention as you do so.

3 After you have written the letter, put it away for a week or so.

4 After this break, set aside 20 minutes and look at the letter once again. Close your eyes and conjure up the person you sent it to in your mind's eye. Imagine their clothes, the texture of their skin, the colour of their eyes, the way they hold themselves and the loving way they look at you.

5 Now imagine stepping into the body of this benevolent being. Leave your own body behind and take on the physical space of this person. See the world through their eyes and see yourself, as you were a moment ago. As you look out of the eyes of this supportive person you may see a younger you standing there, perhaps when you were a child. Just allow whichever image emerges as you see 'yourself' in front of you.

6 Then take some paper and a pen and write a letter back to yourself from the position of this loving and wise person. Answer any questions that were in your original letter and give as much support as you can. Affirm the positive aspects of yourself (refer to the six questions in Exercise 21 above, to remind you) and offer empathy and encouragement.

7 When you have finished the letter, imagine stepping out of the body of the person you chose to support you and return to your own. Take a few deep breaths.

8 Then address an envelope to yourself and put a note in your diary to post the letter from your supporter to yourself in one week from now. When the day arrives, post the letter. In a few days, you'll then receive this letter on your doormat, to read afresh and treasure.

This is a lovely exercise to do when you feel your spirit or your confidence needs a boost, especially if you do not seem to have any friends or family available to support you at that time.

Meeting people and making new friends

There are times in our lives when we can feel very much alone. The death of a loved one or splitting up with a partner can leave us feeling cut off from other people, sometimes even our closest friends. Loneliness can also result from circumstances, such as moving to a new city or country, where friends are no longer near.

When we are in a relationship, we might never mean to drop our friends, but it can often happen. Our social life begins to revolve around our new partner, we have fewer nights out with our mates, we go to events as a couple and spend more evenings at home together without the need for other people. Loneliness can become an issue almost immediately when a relationship of this sort comes to an end. Former friends can all seem to disappear at the same time. Furthermore, there is the awkwardness of friends taking sides and loyalty and embarrassment can split friends into 'mine' and 'yours'. It could be at this point that you realize that you have not made sufficient effort to stay in touch with old friends.

If your relationship ends or you find yourself in a friendless situation for whatever reason, there will come a time when meeting people and making new friends feels important again. This can mean platonic relationships as well as potential romance. You may also want to consider ways of getting back in touch with some of your former friends.

None of this is easy. Making new friends always seems so much simpler when we are younger, as we tend to come across people of a similar age during our normal day-to-day activities, such as school or college. When we are adults, meeting others can feel more contrived as we figure out the kind of people we are looking for, where we are likely to come across them and how to approach them.

Furthermore, the older we get, the more we become entrenched in our distinctive habits and lifestyles. We get choosy about tastes and preferences and are perhaps less flexible and open-minded than we used to be. If we have not been socializing for a while, the thought of having to go out to meet new people can feel daunting, especially if it follows a tragic loss or a situation that has shaken our confidence.

Meeting new people needs a strategy or it can turn into a demoralizing exercise. Start by reflecting on the following questions:

- What kind of person do I want to meet? Am I looking for a potential new partner or a friend?
- Where am I likely to meet someone who has the same interests as I do? (Remember that often our friends have only one or two interests in common with us at first and it is their personality and the dynamic between us that becomes more important later on.)
- What will I do to initiate possible friendship with this person? What will I say? How will I show I'm interested without being too forward?

The following exercise can help you to establish the kind of person you are seeking, where you might find them and how to go about making the right moves.

Exercise 23: Researching former friendships

1 Take a sheet of paper and write down all the friends you currently have, putting each name on a separate line. Add to this all the main friends you have ever had since leaving school or college. A photograph album might help you with this if this is a long period of time or your memory fails you. If you cannot remember exact names do not worry – just put something like 'the guy who played the double-bass' or 'my brother's girlfriend when he was in Sheffield'.

2 Next, write down *where* it was you first met each friend; perhaps it was at a party, a wedding or at a car-maintenance class.

3 Also write down *how* and *why* you became friends – what it was that drew you together (such as 'we both liked the same pop band at college', 'we met at a post-natal clinic' or 'we both shared a passion for travelling abroad').

4 Then look at your list of common interests and places where you met new people and see what themes there are. For example, you may find that you made a number of friends through attending adult education courses over the years, through child-care activities, through clubs, such as cinema or sailing clubs, or through work.

5 Check out how many of these activities you are still interested in, even if you are not actively engaged in them at the moment. Add any other interests that you would like to resume or start from scratch. Think about trying something completely fresh, such as a new sport or fitness activity. Reflect on any groups that might exist in connection with your interests. If you enjoy walking, for example, is there a branch of a hiking association nearby? If you enjoy reading is there a local reading circle, perhaps at your library?

6 Think about all the possible places where other people manage to make friends. Think of how all your friends met *their* friends. Perhaps you know people who met through volunteering for an environmental cause, helping out at a soup kitchen or joining an ice-skating class. See if any of the ways other people seem to make friends holds any appeal for you.

7 Remember too how sometimes the smallest action or being in the right place at the right time can lead to great friendships. I picked up a leaflet once from someone issuing them on the local high street. It led me to join an animal welfare group where I made some wonderful friends I have had for over 15 years. One of them became a boyfriend and another introduced me to the person who became my husband. All from the random act of picking up a leaflet one day on the street! Do not underestimate the wealth of day-to-day opportunities that could lead to significant outcomes.

Getting ready to meet new people

The next step after doing your research into the kinds of people you are likely to find interesting, and where you might find them, is to get out there to meet them. Today might be the day you meet that 'special someone' or a life-long friend. Would you be ready? I have a friend who always has a smart and well-groomed appearance. I once asked him what motivated him to pay so much attention to looking good. He said, 'I want to look my best – you never know who is going to walk around the next corner ...'

Consider the following:

- *Make sure your appearance boosts rather than detracts from your confidence when you go out.* This does not mean spending hours trying to look perfect, but it does mean a certain amount of personal care and hygiene. If you know you look your best, you will feel more self-assured and you will be giving yourself a better chance of responding to, or initiating, encounters in an open and unselfconscious way.

- *Using your findings from the above exercise, start planning and creating opportunities to meet new people.* Do not rely on subscribing to one class a fortnight as your sole chance of meeting someone. Look at every situation involving others as a possible opportunity to make friends. Even if you meet someone you are not particularly interested in, they may have a fascinating sister or brother. Any new person has their own set of friends you could be introduced to. Consider moving beyond your current daily schedule, if it feels limited. For example, if you normally drive to work on your own, join a car-pool, or if you have young children, put up a notice at the crèche to meet other parents at the local park or playground.

  Being self-employed, I usually spend lunchtimes at home on my own. Several years ago, when I was single, I set out one day with the determined goal of having lunch in a local café and speaking to a stranger there. I ordered my meal and then took a look around to see who might be on their own. Before long, I managed to pluck up the courage to talk to a very attractive man on an adjacent table, and we struck up a conversation. He even moved tables to sit with me. We arranged to meet at the same place the following week. Unfortunately at the time, it turned out that he had a girlfriend and did not live in the area, but nevertheless I was extremely pleased with myself for being bold, and gained a renewed confidence about approaching people. Only by going out there, being open and willing to be friendly, will you come across new people who could eventually turn into friends or partners.

- *My advice would be never to join a class or activity with the sole purpose of meeting someone.* Instead, go along to something that you already enjoy and wish to develop in its own right. If you do not choose something you are genuinely interested in you are likely to be bored and frustrated, which will not convey an attractive energy to others. When you are absorbed and enjoy something, you are giving out an aura of interest, satisfaction, fun or joy that other people notice.

- *Be wary of seeming too keen.* Those who appear obviously lonely tend not to be attractive to others. People are often suspicious and wary of someone who is being overly forward or friendly. There seems to be an unspoken social 'pace' for making friends. This usually starts with 'small talk' and shorter impersonal or group encounters, before getting to the point of making special arrangements to meet as individuals. Someone speeding up this process can lead us to feel 'pounced on'; we might doubt their intentions or sense that they must be desperately lonely, and we are likely to respond by hastily retreating.

- *Allow relationships time to grow.* When you look back at the main friendships in your life, reflect on how long they took to develop, from the point of meeting for the first time to being really good friends. Some may have developed quickly, but others may have taken a longer period of time – months or even years – before they felt established. Circumstances can play a part in this; for example, if you attended an intensive residential course for a fortnight, you may have found a new friendship emerged quicker than if you had attended the same course spread over several months.

- *Dinner-dating and speed-dating are popular ways of meeting potential romantic partners.* The advantage they have is that the time allocated with each person is limited, so if there is no spark of interest between you, you can swiftly move on to another person without embarrassment. There is also the opportunity to meet several people at one event, which saves time in comparison to more traditional forms of agency dating.

It is always important to have personal safety in mind when engaging in such activities (and also be aware that serial speed-daters may only be interested in one-night-stands). Letting people know where you are, staying in public places and preparing in advance for getting home safely are essential guidelines. Be wary too of giving strangers your personal details, such as your address and phone number, until you feel you can trust them. The kind of dating where you can be seriously misled is also to be treated with caution, such as on-line chat-rooms via the internet where people can pretend to be anything they want you to believe.

- *Think of some interesting questions to ask others.* Comment on the surroundings or offer a compliment, such as 'That's a great jacket you're wearing.'
- *Remember to be your 'best' self and not a 'false' self when meeting new people* (see Chapters 7 and 8).
- *Finally, do not forget that all of your friends were once complete strangers.* Remember that you found a way to develop those first encounters until those people became friends. If you could do it then, you can do it again.

10

Making changes

Four styles of behaviour

Our behaviour with other people is the outward expression of how we are feeling inside and it directly sends out clues to other people about our level of self-esteem. Our style of behaviour comprises our actions, the way we approach situations, the words we use (and how we say them) and the hidden messages our body gives away. Certain ways of behaving go hand in hand with low or high self-esteem and go on to affect our relationships, as we saw in Chapter 1. In fact, our style of behaviour will affect every relationship we have, whether this involves a partner, parents, children, neighbours, work colleagues, and so on.

There are four main styles of behaviour. Can you see yourself in the examples below? Which style of behaviour do you use most often? Do you swing from one style to another? Try not to judge yourself as you notice and explore this. See the bottom of page 87 to identify the four styles. Tables 4 and 5 (pages 88 and 89) set out the different styles of behaviour in more detail.

Style 1

Your general attitude to other people is to be compliant, to seek approval whenever possible. Your aim is to be liked and you fear any kind of confrontation. You are likely to give in and be submissive. You often find yourself saying phrases such as 'I don't mind', 'What would *you* like to do?' or 'What do *you* suggest?' Your body language is self-conscious; perhaps you fiddle with your hair, cover your mouth or avoid eye contact. Your inner emotions are likely to be fear and anxiety, you 'tread on eggshells' trying to do the 'right thing'.

Style 2

Your general attitude towards others is to get your own way. Life feels like a power struggle you have to win. You shout to get your point across. You can be domineering and hostile at times because people must see that you are in control. You make statements such as: 'Shut up and listen to me', 'I told you so' and 'It's all your fault'.

Your body language involves hands on your hips, folding your arms, frowning or pointing at people. Your inner emotions are likely to be rage and fear – you need people to see who is boss.

Style 3

Your general attitude is to appear to be easygoing and accepting on the surface, but you secretly harbour resentment. You pretend you are fine when you are not; you play down what you want and then feel angry. Deception and manipulation play a hidden part in your interactions with others. You may laugh with others, but say to yourself: 'I'll get you for that', or 'You'll see'. Your body gives false or mixed messages, such as pretending to be relaxed or smiling when your eyes convey cynicism. Emotionally, you are experiencing bitterness, envy and mistrust – you want people to think you are in control, but you are not.

Style 4

Your general attitude is to treat others how you wish to be treated yourself. You are respectful, honest and sincere. You want fair play for everyone. When you are not happy about something you will say so, using phrases such as 'Let's discuss this' and 'How can we resolve this?' You are able to say what you think and to say 'No' when appropriate. Your body language involves direct eye contact and a steady, open posture. Your inner emotions are likely to be self-assured and if you are anxious, you do not mind admitting it. While you might feel apprehensive or nervous about challenges and tricky encounters, you trust that you can cope with most situations, because you are not trying to prove anything.*

What is assertiveness?

Style 4 describes assertive behaviour and is the one that goes hand in hand with high self-esteem. It may surprise you to know that all the other styles depict behaviour from a position of low self-esteem. It is a common misconception that people with aggressive behaviour have high self-esteem. Instead, aggressive behaviour is about attempting to wield power and control over others (superiority),

---

* The styles of behaviour described above are as follows: Style 1 = 'Passive', Style 2 = 'Aggressive', Style 3 = 'Indirectly Aggressive' (also known as 'Passive-Aggressive') and Style 4 = 'Assertive'.

Table 4: Four styles of behaviour

	Assertive	Passive	Aggressive	Indirectly Aggressive
	The Negotiator	The Doormat	The Bully	The Martyr
Attitude	I will stand up for my personal rights and say what I think, while respecting others' right to do the same.	I will not express my thoughts and feelings at all, or so timidly that they can easily be ignored.	I will stand up for what I want at the expense of other people's feelings.	I will pretend I don't mind not expressing myself honestly, but will secretly feel resentful.
Approach	I respect you and hope you can respect me. I will attempt to be as honest as I can be.	I don't count. You can take advantage of me. I don't matter as much as you do.	This is what I think. If you think differently, you are stupid. What I want is more important than what you want.	I'll play down what I want, but you'd better realize that I'll get my revenge if I don't get what I want.
In a crisis	Evaluates situation and takes action based on mutual respect.	Gives in, avoids or withdraws.	Rebels or attacks.	Pretends, manipulates and deceives.
Outcome	We respect each other.	Guilt, anger, frustration.	Hurt, defensive, humiliation.	Avoidance, mistrust.
Intention	Communication and intimacy. To understand and be understood; to give and receive fair play; to negotiate.	To seek approval, be liked, avoid conflict.	To win, if necessary by humiliating or overpowering others, so that they are less able to stand up for themselves.	To deceive and win in the end.

Table 5: Non-verbal behaviour (body language)

Assertive	Passive	Aggressive	Indirectly Aggressive
Relaxed, open, balanced posture.	Slumped, hunched.	Tense, rigid, loud voice.	Sighing, faking being relaxed.
Keeps comfortable distance and respects space of others.	Allows others to invade personal space.	Hand on hips, pointing, glaring.	Two-faced, respectful on the surface.
Direct eye contact.	Avoids eye contact.	Tense jaw and movements.	Mixed messages with body language.
Relaxed, calm voice.	Wobbly, quiet voice.	Loud, harsh voice.	Sarcastic, cynical tone of voice.
Fluent speech.	Throat clearing, 'ums', 'ers', disjointed.	Shouting, finger pointing.	False smiles.
Head held up.	Head lowered, fiddling with hair, covering mouth.	Eyebrows raised in disbelief. Strides around, leans forward.	

whereas people with high self-esteem do not need to prove themselves in this way – they are aiming for equality, not domination. The good news is that you can learn to be assertive and with assertiveness comes better self-esteem, which paves the way towards improved relationships.

Equality and respect are at the heart of assertiveness. Passive, aggressive and indirectly aggressive behaviours involve power and control, not equality. The passive voice whispers: 'I am less important than you, so you can walk all over me.' In a close relationship, this could allow the other person to use and take advantage of you, as you desperately try to be liked and avoid conflict. It could also cause others to see you as one-dimensional, lacking in conviction, imagination or opinions. It is not that you do not have such opinions, but being passive, you rarely give them away for fear of others disagreeing with you.

The aggressive voice yells: 'I need to feel better than you, so I will put you down.' In a romantic relationship this can lead to power struggles, stubbornness and defensiveness. The aggressive person may turn into a 'persecuting' figure, turning their partner into a 'victim'. At its worst this imbalance can result in domestic abuse.

The indirectly aggressive voice says: 'Of course I will smile and agree with you, but I will build up resentment.' In close relationships, this behaviour is likely to lead to mistrust, misunderstandings and second-guessing. Because honesty is being avoided, there will be a lack of directness in the relationship and unresolved issues may never get addressed. Partners may conduct a superficial relationship in this way for years. The indirectly aggressive person may play the role of a 'martyr', but be secretly waiting for recognition and compensation. If they do not receive what they see as their due reward, eventually regret and bitterness can set in, and even revenge.

None of the above behaviours is concerned with respect and fairness. None of them builds trusting, solid relationships. Assertiveness, however, is about putting power and control into balance by aiming to share it equally. It means treating others how you would wish to be treated and respecting yourself in the same way.

Assertive encounters

The main aim of assertiveness is to create as many 'win-win' scenarios as possible with other people. A 'win-win' situation is one where all participants go away feeling good about the interaction. No one feels bullied, or put upon or cheated. Each party feels they have been able to make their point and have been heard. In a 'win-lose' (or 'lose-win') scenario, you or the other person is out to dominate and exert power over the other. One person comes away as the 'victor', the other 'defeated'. This leads to unsuccessful encounters, as the 'winner' always needs to keep winning and the one who is defeated loses self-esteem. The 'lose-lose' scenario is equally unsatisfactory: both parties come away feeling misunderstood or misheard and nothing has been achieved.

Will assertiveness make me selfish?

By creating 'win-win' scenarios, it does not mean we will always get our own way! Part of the philosophy of assertiveness is concerned with fairness for all. This means that sometimes you may have to compromise or negotiate and therefore you do not get everything you want. By acting assertively, however, you balance your own needs and requirements against the needs of others and make a decision based on mutual respect. Assertiveness is about coming from a place of neither superiority nor inferiority, but instead from a place of equality. In this way assertiveness is never 'selfish' – instead it is about being clear about what you want and need, offering others choices, having clear boundaries and being firm.

Developing assertiveness

The following exercises will show you simple steps you can take to start putting assertiveness into practice. Over time, with small changes in behaviour, you are likely to find a positive shift in your handling of situations and increase your self-esteem along the way.

Exercise 24: How to develop assertiveness

1 Think of someone you know who is assertive, such as a relative, friend, or someone at work. It could even be a fictional character from a film or television, or a celebrity. Observe the person and notice what it is about them that is assertive. Make a list of around eight or ten qualities you associate with assertiveness. Notice how this person speaks, what they say, what their intentions seem to be, how their body language reflects assertiveness and any other factors.

2 After observation, you should be building up a picture of what assertiveness looks and sounds like. Next, ask yourself which areas of your life would improve if you were to become more assertive. Be specific, such as: 'I would be able to handle my mother's interference more easily' or 'I'd be more able to ask for what I needed from my partner'. Describe those areas of your life that badly need a more assertive approach. You may wish to see improvements in the way you deal with your family, your partner, children, friends, boss and so on.

The tools below show some useful starting points in developing assertiveness.

Key tools for assertiveness

1 Use the 'broken record' technique. This means that once you have made sure your terms are fair, you state them and stand by them. Always try to include some kind of offer or concession, then repeat your statement over and over without giving in, such as:

'I'm prepared to clear up after you today, but you'll need to do it next time.'
'I won't babysit for you on Saturday, but I am willing to do it on Friday.'

2 When demands are being made of you, use stalling techniques to give yourself time to think, such as:

'I'd like time to think about what you've just said.'
'I'm not sure about that – are you saying ...?' (then repeat what you think you have been asked to do).
'I'm very busy just now. I'll consider what you've said and get back to you.'
'I'm not sure what you're asking – can you please repeat it?'

3 Learn to use 'I feel ...' when you are trying to address a problem with someone, especially your partner. Instead of saying 'You are so mean and horrible to talk about your ex-girlfriend', 'own' your experience and use words such as 'I feel hurt when you talk about your ex-girlfriend'. This means that you are not being accusing and the other person cannot argue about the way you are feeling. It also helps to prevent confrontation and blame.

4 Bear in mind the timing of assertive statements and requests.

Asking your partner to help more with child-care as soon as he or she gets in from work on a Friday evening may not be the best time!

5 Practise and prepare for tricky situations (see Exercise 25 below).

6 Remember to consider:

- Your body language – does it support or detract from what you are trying to say? (Do you have direct eye contact, a relaxed and balanced posture?)
- Your words and how you say them – how much clarity is there, how persistent are you prepared to be?

Exercise 25: Putting assertiveness into practice

1 Make a note of a situation recently where you wish you had been more assertive. Run the scenario through in your mind slowly. Then, using the key tools for assertiveness above, write down the actions you would *like* to have taken, or the words you would like to have said. Start with something very simple, such as telling your partner you do not wish to go to a work party, or admitting that the soup is cold when the waitress asks if the meal is all right.

2 Close your eyes and again, very slowly, re-live the experience in your mind – only this time see yourself putting the new assertive behaviours into practice. Imagine the scenario unfolding like a film. Run through this positive version several times until it feels familiar.

3 Once you feel comfortable, run the scenario through once more and this time practise making your new statements or actions aloud in front of a full-length mirror. This may feel silly at first, but you will need to learn how to speak or act in this new way. It is like learning a new language – you need to do it out loud to get the feel of it. Make sure that you are clear about what you want and how far you will compromise.

4 At the earliest opportunity, try to put your new assertiveness into practice for real when similar scenarios to the one you have rehearsed arise. Allow yourself to be a beginner at this and do not expect too much from yourself too soon.

Ted described his attempt at this exercise in his journal:

There was a situation last week when I wished I had done something differently. My partner accused me of moving an important letter and I knew I had never even seen it. I couldn't get my words out and by the time I'd come to my senses she had stormed off. I felt terrible – like I'd really let myself down.

I explored some ideas for being more assertive and considered how I wished I had responded in this situation. I wish I'd told her, clearly but not rudely, that I had not seen her letter and had certainly not moved it. I would have done this by standing tall and facing her, looking right into her eyes. I would have said something like: 'Debbie, I can assure you that I have not touched your letter.' If she did not back off, I would then say something like: 'I feel unjustly accused, Debs, being attacked like this.'

I practised saying these statements out loud when I was shaving and checked that I was standing in a relaxed and non-defensive way. I felt so confident after several 'rehearsals' that I decided to talk to Debbie about it the very next day. I am glad I did, because in the end she apologized (she'd remembered where she had put the letter) and I felt vindicated and really proud of myself!' (Ted, veterinary nurse, 27)

Now that you are aware of the four different styles of behaving, you can monitor yourself, notice habitual patterns and reflect on the changes you might want to make. Notice too the habitual behaviours of other people: your partner and friends, for example. It could be enlightening to reflect on which styles of behaviour your mother, father or significant carers seemed to express most often when you were growing up. Perhaps you have unconsciously copied someone else's behaviour without realizing the impact it has had on you or on others.

Expect resistance from others

While becoming more assertive is likely to bring improvements in all your relationships, some people may not support you or approve. If for some time you have been passive or a 'people pleaser', for example, certain people around you may have enjoyed the benefits. They may have got their own way or taken advantage of you and could be inconvenienced when you start to stand up for yourself and expect more equal treatment. Likewise, if you have been indirectly aggressive, others may see you becoming more honest and straightforward as you develop assertiveness. This could lead to more real and open encounters that some people may find threatening. You will need to be aware of the impact of making changes and be prepared for the likely reactions.

- What drawbacks do you anticipate by becoming more assertive?
- Who is likely to respond negatively to you being more assertive?
- Which situations do you think will become awkward as a result of your developing assertiveness?
- What problems might follow?

I have seen newly assertive people lose friends, because these so-called 'friends' liked them when they were passive, but found them 'uncooperative' once they became more assertive. If this happens, you will need to decide whether these were true friends in the first place, or people who only liked you because they could get their own way. Losing them may be no bad thing and it gives you space for new friends who share your values about friendship and equality. Exercise 20 on drawing your circle of friends in Chapter 9 may help you through this kind of scenario.

Remember that people who really care for you will want the best for you, and being assertive is a positive and healthy trait. People who are assertive themselves usually appreciate assertiveness in others – they share a common language and common aims.

The assertiveness credo

As you will now realize, being assertive is not just a behaviour, but a philosophy. It promotes beliefs and values about how we and other people should be treated, in as fair and equal a way as possible. Statements such as the ones below reflect this assertiveness philosophy. By accepting and following these beliefs, we see that we are as valuable and worthy as other people and entitled to the same treatment.

- I deserve respect (and so do others).
- I deserve to be treated as an equal (and will treat others as equals, too).

- I am entitled to express my thoughts and feelings (and others are entitled to do so).
- I am entitled to express my opinions and values (and others are entitled to do so).
- I have the right to ask for what I want or need (and others also have this right).
- I am entitled to say that I do not understand (and others are entitled to say so, too).
- I am permitted to make mistakes (and so are others).
- I have the right to change my mind (and others also have this right).
- I am entitled to say 'No' (and so are others).
- I am allowed to be successful (and so are others).

How do you feel about the above statements? Would your self-esteem improve if you were to believe in, and follow, this credo?

The ground rules of assertiveness

Bear in mind the following ground rules for making assertiveness part of your daily life.

1 Remember that the buzz words for assertiveness are 'equality', 'fair play', 'honesty' and 'respect'. These apply as much for yourself as they do for others, meaning you can expect fair play as well as try to offer fair play and you can be respectful to yourself as much as you can offer respect to others. How can you incorporate these elements into your relationship with your partner and others?

2 Good communication is the foundation of assertiveness. Good communication means facing someone and talking things through, being willing to negotiate (but also stating your point of view) and being prepared to compromise (while also standing your ground). It means trying to find a resolution with someone and trying to be as honest as you can be (while also being diplomatic and courteous). How could you improve your communication so that it is more assertive?

3 The equality rule in assertiveness means that if it is acceptable for others to make mistakes, then it is also acceptable for you to make them. It also means that it is not appropriate to have more demanding rules or higher standards for yourself than you have for other people (and vice versa).

11

Improving the bond between you

Being heard

Most of us need to be acknowledged, understood and accepted by others. We are social animals and need interaction, feedback and support. Many features of our twenty-first century lifestyles can prevent these basic needs from being fully met, such as fragmented families, overcrowded cities, increasing interaction with machines instead of people (like computers and television). Often we expend all our energy at work during the day and have nothing left to give to our partners when we come home, or have so many chores there is barely any time left for winding down or debriefing about our day. Yet giving and receiving 'loving attention' is essential to our well-being and crucial to the quality of our relationships.

When we experience our partner truly listening to us and responding honestly and without judgement, something happens to our self-esteem. We usually feel valued for exactly who we are in that moment. When the person listening to us is not trying to make us change, or expecting anything from us, we can feel encouraged to be more honest and can express our feelings and work through them. This is the value of being heard by another.

I have often come across people who expect their partners to be 'mind-readers'. They believe their partner should know what they need, or when something is wrong. They expect their partner to be telepathic. Perhaps they think they have dropped sufficient clues, or assume their partner will think in the same way as they do. Sadly, it is unlikely! It is up to us to let our partners know, and to take more responsibility for what we need. I remember one client who felt that if she had to ask for something from her partner, then it lost its value. We cannot expect our partner to get it right every time. Airing thoughts and feelings helps prevent misunderstandings and unrealistic expectations. Then when your partner next responds without having to be prompted, you will be pleasantly surprised rather than expect this to be the norm.

The listening agreement

My husband and I have an agreement whereby we can request 10 to 20 minutes of pure 'listening time', whenever we need it. This means that all distractions stop (the television is turned off, any papers or books are put down, the answerphone is switched on) and one of us expresses his or her feelings, worries or doubts to the other, who listens very carefully, without interrupting. One of us might need to let off steam about an incident at work, for example, or tell the other something they are unhappy about in the relationship. If there is an issue that needs discussing, we can then reverse the roles so that the concern can be fully aired.

This method ensures that we always know that we can find time to be heard by each other. It means we do not have to hide concerns, store them up inside, or brood on them. We have established an acceptance that allows any concerns, no matter how painful or difficult, to be aired. When we do this, we inevitably feel closer.

Exercise 26: Try the 20-minute listening agreement

We can offer loving attention to those we care about by developing our ability to listen well and focusing wholeheartedly on what the other person is trying to convey. We can learn to listen without judging and to encourage someone to explore and express their feelings. We will then be able to understand them better (as they start to understand themselves more) and become closer to them. When you next feel the need to air your feelings to your partner, try the following:

1 Set aside 10–20 minutes, when you have a little time for relaxation together. (If your life is so busy that you cannot find this time together, I would encourage you to address this as a matter of urgency.)

2 Ask your partner to 'just listen' to what you have to say. Ask for no interrupting, criticizing, giving advice, 'rescuing' or having their say, even if they disagree or get upset with what you are saying.

3 Invite your partner to do the same, either at the same time or at another time when he or she needs to talks things through.

My husband and I regularly go for long walks at the weekend and part of this time has become an opportunity to air any issues or problems between us. We call it our time for 'unfinished business' and perhaps to mention any mini-resentments, grievances, niggles or concerns. We also tell each other about the special things we have appreciated about each other, and show our gratitude. By doing this regularly, no minor concerns are ever allowed to build into anything unmanageable.

The following exercise is a particularly rewarding one to do on an anniversary or birthday or any other time when you want to celebrate your relationship.

Exercise 27: Appreciating each other

1 Find some special time when you can be alone together, perhaps when you are dining out, going for a stroll, sitting in a park or watching a sunset.

2 Find five things about your partner that you appreciate, at least one of which must be a *new* appreciation, something you have never mentioned before. You might include the ways in which he or she has been supportive, has brought joy to your life or shown little tokens of love. Try to refer to specific incidents where you valued your partner, or any moments that made you smile or feel close. Share your list with your partner.

3 Then sit back and receive five compliments or appreciative comments from your partner!

This is a wonderfully affirming way for both of you to feel special and to show your gratitude.

'Loving attention'

As well as the '20-minute listening' agreement, we can learn to offer 'loving attention' in other ways to people we care about. 'Loving attention' happens during a conversation when we follow a person's flow of thinking, giving them time and encouragement to explore and express themselves in as much detail as they wish to. Here are examples of two kinds of interacting. One is with 'loving attention', the other is without it:

Example 1:

Karen: Hi, Derek, how's it going?
Derek: Oh, you know – not so bad . . . (looks sad).
Karen: (fails to notice that anything is wrong) Well, I'm off to college in a few weeks.
Derek: Yeah – I thought college was great when I was there (putting on a brave face).
Karen: Do you want to go for a drink later?
Derek: Er, no, I'm a bit busy at the moment (wants to avoid further meaningless contact).
Karen: Right, well, I'll see you around . . .

In this example, Karen has missed the opportunity to help Derek to explore his feelings. Maybe she needed clearer signals of distress from him. If Derek had explained that he was feeling 'out of sorts', perhaps she might have helped him to explore his emotions. As it was, in this example, neither person reached out to the other.

Example 2:

Clara: Hi, Dave, how's it going?
Dave: Oh, you know – not so bad . . .
Clara: (notices he looks sad) You look like something's bothering you – do you want to talk about it?
Dave: (sighs) Well, yeah, I wasn't going to mention it, but you're right, I'm feeling really rough today. In fact, I've been like this for the last two weeks.
Clara: (gets closer to him to make full eye contact and to show she is interested) What's happening?
Dave: I've been feeling depressed and sort of angry and I don't know why. I haven't mentioned it to anyone. I feel a bit pathetic to be honest.
Clara: It sounds like it's really troubling you – and you don't really know what's causing it?
Dave: That's it. I seem to be getting in a rage, at myself and anyone else I come across, and I feel so miserable when I wake up.

Clara: That must be really hard to deal with . . . and it started about two weeks ago (stops to think). Has anything changed recently? (helping him to explore).

Dave: Not that I can think of . . . (reflects) except, yes, there is something about this time of year which bugs me. The beginning of March is when my mother died, but that was years ago.

Clara: It might be years ago, but it still means something.

Dave: Yeah – I feel like crying right now . . . (starts to express his sadness and grief).

Dave feels listened to, understood and accepted by Clara. At another time, Dave will be able to offer Clara the same kind of 'loving attention'.

You might want to reflect on the kinds of conversations you have had recently with your partner. Have you offered each other the space and encouragement to talk feelings through, or have you cut each other off, because you had 'better' things to do? Have you both been too busy to stop and listen to each other – or even to notice if there is something wrong? What kind of difference would it make to your relationship if you both were to include more room for loving attention? Do you need to re-prioritize some of your activities, so that you can give more time to your relationship?

Sex

This book focuses more on the emotional aspects of relationships than the physical, but no book of this sort would be satisfactory without giving sex a mention. The difficulty with sex, especially in the West, is that so few people talk about it that it becomes something hidden and often subversive or shameful. It is also difficult for us to know if our sex lives are 'normal', because genuine information is rarely shared. Magazines may tell us national averages regarding the frequency of making love, or preferred sexual activities, but this leads us to compare ourselves with a so-called 'norm' and can leave us feeling inadequate or abnormal.

The greatest factor influencing sex between couples is sexual compatibility. It does not matter whether, in terms of 'national averages', you and your partner fit the patterns or not. What matters most is whether you both feel comfortable with the way sex expresses itself in your relationship. It is unlikely that two people will share exactly the same sexual libido, needs or desires, but a close degree of compatibility means that both of you can respond to the preferences of the other without causing too many problems. Sexual compatibility is something you will discover and can adjust to (like everything else), as you progress through the various stages of your relationship.

Sex, power and self-esteem can be closely linked in relationships. At its worst, sex can be used as a bargaining tool, a means of manipulating, punishing or dominating the other. It can be the cause of degradation, fear and inadequacy and because it is not often discussed between partners or close friends, we might feel alone and unsure about whether our sex life is healthy for us.

The same guidelines regarding honesty and expressing our genuine feelings apply around sexual matters. If someone cares deeply for us, our views about sex, like anything else, will be respected and honoured. The most important piece of advice therefore is to try to talk with your partner about your sex life. Discuss your views, your preferences and your fears at quiet, close times together. It may be easier to do this when you are not being sexual together or about to engage in sexual activity. Try to share your feelings about sex with each other in an accepting way, so that you can learn and adjust to each other.

In the final chapter, you can discover how to sustain high self-esteem and how to feel as good about yourself as you possibly can.

12

Feeling good about yourself

When we feel good about ourselves we project this out into the world and appear energetic, confident and attractive to other people. Taking the time to ensure we feel as good about ourselves as we can will give us a head start when we are looking for a partner, or hoping to sustain a relationship we already have.

Feeling good about yourself will be a unique formula applicable only to you. For some people, being slim and fit helps them to feel at their best. Others might need to know that they are contributing, being creative, being true to their purpose or achieving goals or status to feel positive about themselves. The following exercise will help you to see what are the important factors that contribute to your sense of self-worth and confidence.

Exercise 28: The fulfilment chart

1 On a sheet of paper (graph paper is preferable) draw a line along the bottom and a line up the left-hand side to form a large 'L' shape.

2 List all the factors that are important to you in your life, and in particular, to your self-esteem. You might choose from the following, or use your own labels. Select as many as are applicable (the order is not important) and write them under the horizontal line (see Figure 7).

> work/career, family, love-life or main relationship, social life or friends, travel and tourism, health, fitness, diet, leisure/hobbies, personal development, self-care, spiritual development, religion, studying/learning, creativity, nature, entertainment, contribution (such as your appreciation of others, donations, voluntary work, helping others in trouble and so on)

3 Then use your judgement to give each factor a self-esteem rating out of 10 (where 0 is 'very poor' and 10 is 'excellent') to measure how well that area is working in your life at present. Show your measurement on the graph, using the vertical scale.

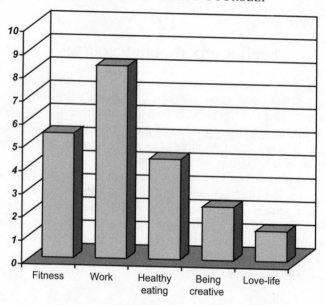

Figure 7: The fulfilment chart

4 Look at each factor and ask yourself the following: 'Is this factor helping me to feel as good as I can about myself? Does it need more attention or time? Am I neglecting this important element in my life?'

5 Once you have completed your graph, you will get a picture of how fulfilled your life is at the moment (the higher the scores, the more satisfied you are with your life). The graph will show you which areas you may need to focus on to bring more self-esteem and balance into your life and which areas are working well as they are.

6 The next stage is to take the first factor on your graph and, no matter what actual score you gave it, imagine being able to give it a score of 10 ('excellent'). Reflect on that life-area and decide *what you would have to be doing differently* in order to reach a score of 10. Write these ideas down. For example, for 'fitness' you might currently give yourself a score of 5, because you do a long cycle ride once a week and play football now and again. You might decide you could raise your fitness score from 5 to 10 by making the journey to work by bicycle instead of on the bus, by playing hockey with your workmates one evening a week and by offering to coach your son's football team on a Saturday morning.

If you find it hard to imagine what a score of 10 would consist of, try doing this part of the exercise using small increments (for example, if you scored 5, what would need to happen in order to get to 6?). Keep going up the scale in this way until you reach a score of 10.

7 Do this same process with each of the bars on your chart. Describe what would be happening in each life-area if you truly made the most of it and lived it to its fullest.

8 Then list five small actions or steps you intend to take this week in one or more life-areas to make some improvements. Set yourself specific tasks, with dates if possible.

This is a useful exercise to do every six months or so to make sure you are on track with what you need to be doing to maintain your self-esteem at a high level and make the most of your life.

Your 10-point self-esteem plan

Most of us know that certain things need to be in place in our lives in order for our self-esteem to be high. Perhaps we need to be 'doing' certain activities to feel good about ourselves, or achieving, or earning a certain amount of money. I recall a client who needed to start her day with a two-mile run in order to feel positive about herself for the rest of the day. She knew that if she achieved very little else that day, at least she had done her run. Another client needed to write at least 500 words of his novel each evening to reach the feeling that his day had been worthwhile. Or maybe your self-esteem is more dependent on your looks or on getting along well with other people. Like the fulfilment chart above, the 10 points of your 'self-esteem requirements' will be unique to you.

Exercise 29: Drawing up your 10-point self-esteem plan

In order to draw up your individual 10-point self-esteem plan, you will need to take some time to reflect on your past history.

1 Think back in your life to times when you felt completely positive about yourself. These will be moments when you felt an inner worthiness and confidence. Perhaps they are times when you conquered something, won or achieved something great, proved yourself or made a difference to someone's life. Try to find about five of these highly charged experiences from your past.

2 Now close your eyes and visualize each experience and the feelings that went with it. Allow yourself to feel the sense of pride and self-belief, the excitement of success or the glow of compassion and benevolence.

3 Imagine stepping into the body of the person you were then. Imagine taking up the space of that joyful person from your past. Re-live the situation, feel the energy of it in your body, see the world through the eyes of that younger you. Remember that this was you and no one else, and you can reach this feeling again.

4 When you have rediscovered those strong, affirming feelings, label them and write them down. They might include feeling bold, brave, an inner strength, calm, determination, certainty. Take a look at your current lifestyle and think about what you would need to be doing now to attain those feelings again.

5 Make a list of ten activities – attitudes, goals, risks or successes – that could lead you to feeling that way again. Be precise and look at the broad spectrum of your life. Your 10-point plan needs to be such that if you were to follow it, it would guide you daily towards increased self-esteem and greater happiness.

This is my current 10-point self-esteem plan (in no particular order):

1 Sustaining a great relationship with my husband.
2 Having a good balance between seeing friends and time to myself.
3 Making a difference to people through my work.
4 Maintaining a good professional reputation.
5 Continuing to get my writing published.
6 Being creative and inventive in my life and work.
7 Getting regular exercise in a variety of ways.
8 Eating lots of vegetables and fruit.
9 Taking care of my health and appearance.
10 Staying trim.

6 Once you have drawn up your own 10-point plan, take each point in turn and explore how it would look at its worst and at its best. Consider what you would be doing and how you would be feeling if this area was generating low self-esteem at one extreme and high self-esteem at the other. The examples below should help you.

6 Being creative and inventive in my life and work.

At worst (low self-esteem) <------------------>	At best (high self-esteem)
Being in a rut in my daily schedule.	Being spontaneous.
Being lazy and using old formulas in my work.	Getting creative stimulation from books and courses.
Being isolated as a self-employed person.	Networking and building new contacts.

9 Taking care of my health and appearance.

At worst (low self-esteem) <------------------>	At best (high self-esteem)
Eating when not hungry.	Watching what I eat.
Not bothering to exercise.	Commitment to regular fun exercise.
Wearing frumpy clothes.	Wearing elegant clothes.

By identifying where you might go wrong (low self-esteem) and how to succeed (high self-esteem) in each area, you should now be in a strong position to see what you need to be doing to sustain a high level of self-esteem in the long term.

I know that I need to keep focusing on this plan in order for my well-being and self-esteem to remain at a high level. If I neglect or suffer a setback in any area, I need to make the effort to redress the balance and make sure each area is working at optimum level once again.

Remember too that your 10-point plan will probably change over time, so you may wish to revisit this exercise every six months or so to keep it relevant and up to date.

Once you have got to grips with the format of the 10-point plan, you can use it to draw up a plan for your relationship. If you are single you might wish to draw up a plan for meeting someone new and if you are currently in a relationship, you might look at a plan to sustain it.

Exercise 30: Your 10-point plan for meeting someone new

Your plan will be designed to help you optimize your chances of meeting a new potential partner. Hopefully, you will have already identified some useful steps you could take in this respect from previous exercises. Collect these ideas together now to create your 10-point plan. It might look something like this:

1 Check my address book and send a card or email to someone I have lost contact with who used to be a friend.

2 Make the effort to arrange to see current friends. Get actual dates in the diary, even if only provisional.

3 Join a club or group where I'm likely to meet people with similar interests.

4 Organize a social gathering (for neighbours or work colleagues) or a theme party for friends, or a party for only my single friends, where each person has to bring along someone I've not met.

5 Take a risk and try a new activity involving others (if I don't like it, I don't have to go back).

6 Expand my comfort zone and smile at anyone I find attractive this week, to see what it feels like.

7 Practise some opening lines for starting conversations with people.

8 Dare to speak to someone I don't know (in a safe setting), like at work, in a café, at the library.

9 Investigate local dinner-dating or speed-dating.

10 Find a single friend or colleague I can go with to a dinner-date or speed-dating.

This time, instead of reflecting on what might happen if you do not put these guiding principles into practice, focus fully on committing to taking these actions to take you nearer to your goal.

If you are currently in a relationship you would like to sustain, then do the following exercise.

Exercise 31: Your 10-point plan for enhancing your relationship

This exercise will help you to focus on your relationship and list the ten crucial factors to bear in mind to help your relationship work better.

1 Think back to the most successful and loving times in your current (or past) relationship.

2 Identify the special moments that worked well, what was happening and what it was you did to help create them. Write the scenarios down.

3 Then start putting together a list of ten points that you believe would help your relationship to work at its best. Think about what you want to bring to the relationship. Consider your approach to your partner, how you treat him or her, how you express love and demonstrate elements such as respect, trust and thoughtfulness. (Remember that you cannot expect the other person to act in any particular way; you can only decide to make changes in your own attitudes and behaviour.)

My current 10-point relationship plan (with my husband) looks like this:

1 Taking the trouble to plan 'dates' together.
2 Finding ways to show my love and appreciation, in some small way, every day.
3 Remembering (and applying) the 'style of loving' he prefers most (see Chapter 6).
4 Being attentive to his needs, especially when he's tired.
5 Doing little tasks for him, so he doesn't have to bother with them.
6 Welcoming him when he comes home from work each night.
7 Putting his choice of radio station/TV programme/leisure pursuit before mine more often.
8 Finding time for a '20-minute listening agreement' whenever he needs it (see Chapter 11).
9 Giving him space alone when he needs it.
10 Preparing special surprises for birthday, anniversary and festive celebrations.

4 Then decide what you will do today to enhance your relationship and help it to blossom.

The miracle question

The 'miracle question' is a technique devised by Steve de Shazer (referred to in his book *Clues: Investigating Solutions in Brief*

Therapy, New York, W.W. Norton, 1988). The exercise takes around ten minutes. Ensure that you will not be distracted. Get comfortable, sitting or lying down, and have a pen and paper handy. When you are ready, look at the following scenario.

Exercise 32: Asking the miracle question

Imagine that during the night some amazing miracle happened and the next morning you woke up with a huge dose of self-esteem. You might imagine that you were given a painless and secret injection of a magical 'self-esteem potion' during the night, or that some transformation took place inside you. All your circumstances stay the same; the only difference is that you wake up a much more self-confident and self-assured person.

Close your eyes and see if, in your mind's eye, you can imagine the feeling of waking up full of self-esteem. You do not need to worry about how this could possibly have happened, just focus on what it would *feel* like inside your body and your mind. As you immerse yourself in this experience, open your eyes briefly to look at each question and then go back into your reverie with your eyes closed. Answer the questions in as much detail as you can.

1 As you wake up with a greater sense of self-esteem, what would your first *thoughts* be?

2 How would you *know* that you had more self-esteem?

3 How would you *start* the day?

4 What *new approach* would you have? (for example: 'I'd be less self-critical', 'I'd feel less threatened by others', 'I'd be kinder to myself').

5 What would you be doing *differently*?

6 How would *your partner or others* know you had more self-esteem? What would they see *different* in you? How might they react?

7 How would you regard your partner and your relationship from this position of high self-esteem? (If you do not have a partner, how would you feel about being in a new relationship?)

8 What *changes* would you want to make in your relationship? What would you change *first*? (If you do not have a partner, how could you be in a better position to meet someone suitable? What would you address *first*?)

9 Which are the easiest, or most straightforward, aspects of this 'new you' that you could *put into practice*?

10 What would your *first step* be?

The power of this exercise rests on being able to create a vision of your new self. It is very important for us, when embarking on any kind of change, to have an idea of where we are heading and to start *to feel* what that might be like. If we can step into the experience of being ourselves with more self-esteem (even if we do not know how we got there), we get a genuine flavour of what it means to have more self-esteem. We can visualize this new self and 'try it on for size' and feel what would be different about who we are.

It is also important to do this kind of exercise to see if we *like* the person we think we want to become. This kind of technique can bring to light hidden blocks and resistances that may have been secretly preventing us from becoming this new self.

If you are pleased and comfortable with the new you with more self-esteem, make a clear statement to yourself that you are going to put one or two aspects of this new self into practice, as soon as possible. This could mean changing something about your body language, the way you speak to people, your eye contact or the kind of inner dialogue you have with yourself. Alternatively, it could be a shift in how you dress, your expectations of others or yourself, or the way you take care of yourself. It might even mean no longer putting up with being treated in a certain way in your relationship or making some views, opinions or needs known to your partner. Whatever changes you make are going to stand you in good stead for your current or future relationships.

A final word about self-esteem

It is easy to imagine that people with high self-esteem are somehow able to rise above the trials and tribulations life seems to throw at everyone else. However, high self-esteem does not mean being armed against the world and immune to problems and upsets. People with high self-esteem still have difficulties, get let down or make terrible mistakes, but they allow themselves to experience all the feelings that are involved, and have better ways of bouncing back from disasters.

People with high self-esteem honour the whole range of human emotions that well up when they face situations that bring sadness, fear, hurt or anger, and they look after themselves as they experience those feelings. They know how to pick themselves up after a setback by being a good friend to themselves. When they perform less well than they had hoped, they find out what is wrong and how to put it right without berating themselves. They know how to congratulate themselves when they score a success. High self-esteem is not about getting everything right, but about reminding ourselves that we are still learning and giving ourselves permission to try again.

Now that you are at the end of this book, you will know more about the key qualities that make healthy relationships, such as respect, equality, honesty, trust, assertiveness, intimacy, good communication skills, compatibility and, of course, self-esteem. I trust you will be more aware of the ingredients that go towards creating strong, lasting relationships and where you might have been going wrong in the past. I hope too that you will have identified many ways in which you can enhance your self-esteem and can now feel entirely worthy and deserving of your ultimate goal – a loving relationship.

Further Help

If you need more help working through relationship issues, either with a partner or on your own, please consider seeing a counsellor. The British Association for Counselling and Psychotherapy provides lists of counsellors in each area of the country. You can telephone them or refer to the register on their website. BACP is based at 35–37 Albert Street, Rugby, Warwickshire, CV21 2SG, telephone 0870 443 5252. Visit their website at www.bacp.co.uk or email them on bacp@bacp.co.uk

Alison's website is at www.awaines.fsnet.co.uk, email alison@awaines.fsnet.co.uk

Suggested Reading

Briggs Myers, Isabel, *Gifts Differing*, Consulting Psychologists Press, Inc., 1980.

Dickson, Anne, *A Woman in your own Right*, Quartet Books, 1983.

Glass, Lilian, *Attracting Terrific People*, Thorsons, 1998.

Gray, John, *Men are from Mars, Women are from Venus*, HarperCollins, 2003.

Lindenfield, Gael, *Super Confidence,* Thorsons, 1989.

Litvinoff, Sarah, *The Relate Guide to Better Relationships,* Vermillion, 1998.

Litvinoff, Sarah, *The Relate Guide to Starting Again,* Vermillion, 1993.

Norwood, Robin, *Women Who Love Too Much*, Arrow, 1985.

Rogers, Carl R., *A Way of Being*, Mariner Books, 1995.

Skynner, Robin and Cleese, John, *Families and How to Survive them*, Mandarin, 1983.

Stafford, David and Hodgkinson, Liz, *Codependency: How to Break Free and Live Your Own Life*, Piatkus, 1991.

Waines, Alison, *The Self-Esteem Journal: Using a Journal to Build Self-Esteem*, Sheldon Press, 2004.